Highbury to Emirates: The Arsenal Football Club Story

Gigi Romano

Title: Highbury to the Emirates: The Arsenal Football Club Story

Author: Gigi Romano

© 2024. **Gigi Romano. All rights reserved.**

No part of this book may be reproduced, distributed, or transmitted in any form or by any means, including photocopying, recording, or other electronic or mechanical methods, without the prior written permission of the publisher, except in the case of brief quotations embodied in critical reviews and certain other noncommercial uses permitted by copyright law. For permission requests, write to the publisher, addressed "Attention: Permissions Coordinator," at the address below.

Disclaimer:

The information in this book is provided for informational purposes only. The author and publisher have made every effort to ensure the accuracy of the information within, but the information contained herein is provided "as is" without warranty, either express or implied. The author and publisher shall not be liable for any losses or damages resulting from the use of the information contained in this book.

First Edition: August, 2024

Contents

Chapter 1: The Birth of Dial Square (1886)
Chapter 2: From Dial Square to Royal Arsenal (1887-1891)
Chapter 3: Professionalism and Growth (1891-1893)
Chapter 4: Woolwich Arsenal and Financial Struggles (1893-1904)
Chapter 5: The Move to Highbury (1904-1913)
Chapter 6: World War I and Its Impact (1914-1919)
Chapter 7: The Controversial Promotion (1919)
Chapter 8: The Chapman Revolution Begins (1925-1930)
Chapter 9: The First Taste of Glory (1930-1933)
Chapter 10: The Sudden Loss of Chapman (1934)
Chapter 11: The Road to War (1936-1939)
Chapter 12: The Immediate Post-War Period (1945-1950)
Chapter 13: A Declining Force (1951-1958)
Chapter 14: Searching for Stability (1958-1966)
Chapter 15: The Bertie Mee Era Begins (1966-1970)
Chapter 16: The Double of 1971
Chapter 17: Post-Double Decline (1972-1976)
Chapter 18: FA Cup Success and European Nights (1977-1979)
Chapter 19: The Early Graham Years (1986-1989)
Chapter 20: The 1989 Title Triumph
Chapter 21: Continued Success and Controversies (1990-1993)
Chapter 22: The Post-Graham Transition (1994-1996)
Chapter 23: Return to Silverware (2014-2017)
Chapter 24: The Final Years of Wenger (2017-2018)
Chapter 25: The Unai Emery Era (2018-2019)
Chapter 27: Building for the Future (2020-2022)
Chapter 28: Arsenal's Resurgence (2022-Present)
Chapter 29: The Foundation of Arsenal Women (1987-1992)
Chapter 30: Dominance in Women's Football (1993-2007)
Chapter 31: Arsenal Women in the Modern Era (2008-Present)
Chapter 32: Community and Charity Work
Chapter 33: Arsenal's Global Fanbase
Chapter 34: Arsenal in Popular Culture
Chapter 35: Arsenal's All-Time Legends
Chapter 36: Records and Achievements
Chapter 37: Arsenal's Future
Appendices
Appendix A: Complete List of Arsenal Managers
Appendix B: Statistical Records
Appendix C: Arsenal in European Competitions
References and Further Reading

Chapter 1: The Birth of Dial Square (1886)

Origins of the Club: The Formation by Munitions Workers in Woolwich

In the latter half of the 19th century, the British Empire was at its zenith, and with it came a burgeoning industrial landscape. Woolwich, a district in southeast London, was home to the Royal Arsenal, the epicenter of British munitions production. Within the walls of this vast complex, thousands of workers toiled, many of whom had been drawn from different parts of the country by the promise of steady work and a better life. Amidst the clang of machinery and the grind of daily labor, a sense of camaraderie grew among these men, many of whom were passionate about football, a sport rapidly gaining popularity across England.

The idea of forming a football club was born out of this shared passion. In the autumn of 1886, a group of these workers, led by David Danskin, a Scotsman with a love for the game, and Jack Humble, another influential figure, decided to create a football team that would allow them to play the sport they loved on a more organized basis. These men were not just colleagues but friends, united by a common purpose. They pooled their resources—Danskin himself contributed 3 shillings, and others chipped in smaller amounts—to purchase a football, and thus, Dial Square Football Club was born.

The name "Dial Square" was inspired by one of the workshops within the Royal Arsenal complex, where many of these men worked. This workshop was known for the large sundial that adorned its entrance, a symbol of time and precision, fitting for the hardworking individuals who decided to use its name as a badge of honor for their fledgling football club.

The First Match: Dial Square's Inaugural Game and Its Significance

The newly formed Dial Square team wasted little time in organizing their first match. On December 11, 1886, they traveled to the Isle of Dogs to face Eastern Wanderers, a local side. The journey to this first match was an adventure in itself, with the team traveling by horse-drawn carriage and ferry, reflecting the rudimentary nature of travel at the time.

The match was played on a foggy afternoon, typical of London in winter. Despite the conditions, the team, wearing makeshift kits of red shirts—a color chosen because it was the most readily available—triumphed with a resounding 6-0 victory. This result was more than just a win; it was a statement of intent.

The men of Dial Square had not only formed a team but had proven themselves on the pitch, laying down the first brick in what would become one of the most storied football clubs in history.

This match also signified the growing popularity of football among the working class. It was a sport that provided an escape from the drudgery of industrial labor, offering both physical release and the opportunity to forge a collective identity. For the Dial Square players, their inaugural game was a moment of pride and a glimpse into the future potential of their club.

Early Organizational Structure: The Founding Members and Initial Management

In the weeks and months following their first match, the men of Dial Square set about formalizing their club. David Danskin was naturally chosen as the first captain due to his leadership qualities and his pivotal role in founding the team. Jack Humble, who would later become one of the most important figures in the club's early history, was also instrumental in these formative days.

The early management of Dial Square was a collective effort. Decisions were made democratically, with all members having a say in the club's affairs. There were no grand plans or visions of future glory—only the simple desire to play football and compete. They adopted an informal but effective approach to management, focusing on organizing matches, securing a steady stream of players, and ensuring the club's financial stability, albeit on a very modest scale.

At this stage, the club had no formal home ground. Matches were arranged on available public fields, with home games often played at the Manor Field in Plumstead, a common playing ground for many local teams. The players themselves took on multiple roles, from organizing fixtures to maintaining equipment, embodying the spirit of a true grassroots club.

As 1886 drew to a close, Dial Square was not yet a household name, even within their local community. However, the foundations had been laid, and the club had already established a reputation for its competitive spirit and unity. The story of Dial Square was just beginning, with the coming years set to bring about significant changes and a transformation into the club that would later become known as Arsenal.

Chapter 2: From Dial Square to Royal Arsenal (1887-1891)

Name Change and Expansion: Transition from Dial Square to Royal Arsenal

By the start of 1887, the men behind Dial Square realized that their club needed a name that better reflected their origins and ambitions. The name Dial Square was intimately connected to a small section of the Royal Arsenal, but as the club began to grow, there was a desire to adopt a name that would resonate more broadly with the community. The decision was made to rename the club "Royal Arsenal," a title that carried the weight and prestige of the munitions factory that employed them.

The name change was more than symbolic. It marked the beginning of a new phase for the club, one that saw increased organization and a clearer identity. Royal Arsenal was a name that not only acknowledged the club's roots but also aligned it with the power and authority associated with the Royal Arsenal complex, one of the most important industrial sites in the British Empire.

With the new name came expansion. The club began to attract more players, many of whom were also employed at the Royal Arsenal. This influx of talent allowed the club to field more competitive teams and to participate in a broader range of matches. The early years of Royal Arsenal were characterized by a growing sense of ambition, as the club sought to establish itself not just as a recreational team but as a formidable force in local football.

Early Competitions: Participation in Local Leagues and Cup Competitions

As Royal Arsenal grew in stature, so too did their ambitions on the pitch. The club began to enter local competitions, with the aim of proving their mettle against more established teams. One of the first significant competitions they entered was the Kent Senior Cup, which was open to teams from across the region. Though success in these early competitions was limited, participation was crucial in raising the profile of the club and providing valuable experience to the players.

In addition to local cups, Royal Arsenal also began competing in friendly matches against other prominent teams in London and the surrounding areas. These games were often fiercely contested and provided the club with the opportunity to gauge their progress against strong opposition. Matches against clubs like Millwall Rovers (later Millwall FC) were particularly significant, as they helped to foster early rivalries that would endure for decades.

The club's participation in these early competitions and friendlies was a crucial step in their development. It provided the players with the opportunity to hone their skills and tactics in a competitive environment, while also exposing the club to a wider audience. Each match was a learning experience, and though trophies were hard to come by in these early years, the groundwork was being laid for future success.

First Home Grounds: Early Playing Fields and Stadium Arrangements

During this period of expansion, finding a suitable and consistent home ground became a priority for Royal Arsenal. The club's early years had been characterized by a nomadic existence, with matches played on various fields around Woolwich and Plumstead. However, as the club grew, the need for a permanent home became increasingly apparent.

One of the first significant grounds that Royal Arsenal called home was the Manor Ground in Plumstead. This venue, which the club began using in the late 1880s, provided a more stable base for their operations. The Manor Ground was a modest facility, with basic amenities, but it represented a step up from the informal fields that had previously hosted their matches.

The move to the Manor Ground was significant for several reasons. Firstly, it provided the club with a dedicated venue for both matches and training, which was essential for the development of the team. Secondly, it allowed the club to generate more income through gate receipts, as the ground could accommodate a larger number of spectators. This financial boost was crucial in funding the club's activities and securing its future.

However, the Manor Ground was not without its challenges. The pitch was often in poor condition, particularly during the winter months, and the facilities were basic at best. Despite these issues, the ground became synonymous with Royal Arsenal during these formative years, serving as the backdrop for many of the club's early triumphs and setbacks.

As Royal Arsenal continued to evolve, so too did their ambitions. The transition from Dial Square to Royal Arsenal was more than just a change of name; it was a transformation in identity and purpose. The club was no longer a simple group of workers playing for recreation; it was becoming a serious footballing entity with aspirations that extended far beyond the confines of Woolwich. The foundation had been laid, and the stage was set for the next chapter in the club's history—a chapter that would see Royal Arsenal rise to even greater heights and begin the journey towards becoming one of England's most storied football clubs.

Chapter 3: Professionalism and Growth (1891-1893)

Turning Professional: The Decision to Turn Professional and Its Implications

By the early 1890s, football in England was undergoing a transformation. The sport was growing rapidly, with clubs increasingly viewing football as a professional endeavor rather than just a pastime. Royal Arsenal, which had already established itself as a formidable amateur club, began to grapple with the decision to turn professional. This was a crucial juncture in the club's history, one that would set the course for its future.

The push towards professionalism was driven by several factors. Firstly, the success and popularity of Royal Arsenal had attracted talented players from across the region, many of whom were being tempted by professional contracts offered by other clubs. To retain these players and continue competing at a high level, Royal Arsenal needed to offer competitive wages, which necessitated a shift to professionalism.

Secondly, the financial realities of running a football club were becoming increasingly apparent. Gate receipts were an important source of revenue, but they were not enough to cover the growing expenses associated with maintaining a competitive team. Turning professional would allow the club to operate on a more sustainable financial footing, enabling them to invest in players, facilities, and infrastructure.

The decision to turn professional was not taken lightly. It required a fundamental shift in the club's operations, moving from a volunteer-based model to a more structured, business-oriented approach. This included formalizing player contracts, establishing a more rigorous training regime, and hiring staff to manage the club's day-to-day operations.

In 1891, Royal Arsenal officially became a professional football club. This marked the beginning of a new era, one that would see the club transition from a local amateur team to a significant force in English football. The move to professionalism also had broader implications, as it placed Royal Arsenal in a stronger position to compete with other professional clubs and attracted more fans to their matches.

Joining the Football League: Entry into the Second Division

Following the decision to turn professional, Royal Arsenal set its sights on joining the Football League, the premier competition for professional football clubs in England. At the time, the Football League consisted of two divisions: the First Division, which featured the top clubs in the country, and the Second Division, which was a proving ground for clubs aspiring to reach the top tier.

In 1893, Royal Arsenal was accepted into the Second Division of the Football League, becoming the first club from the south of England to join the competition. This was a significant achievement, as it marked the club's entry into the national football scene and provided an opportunity to compete against some of the best teams in the country.

Joining the Football League brought with it a new set of challenges. The competition was fierce, with clubs from across the country vying for promotion to the First Division. Royal Arsenal faced the task of proving themselves against more established teams, many of which had been playing professional football for several years.

The move to the Football League also required the club to adapt to a more demanding schedule. The league format meant that Royal Arsenal would be playing regular fixtures against strong opposition, requiring greater consistency and resilience from the players. The club's management also had to ensure that they were financially viable, as participation in the Football League brought increased costs, including travel expenses and player wages.

Despite these challenges, joining the Football League was a critical step in the club's development. It provided Royal Arsenal with the platform to showcase their talents on a national stage and laid the groundwork for their future success.

Initial League Campaigns: Performance in the Early Football League Years

Royal Arsenal's debut season in the Second Division of the Football League was a momentous occasion for the club. The 1893-94 season saw the team face a steep learning curve as they adjusted to the rigors of league football. The competition was intense, with matches often characterized by physical play and tactical battles.

In their first season, Royal Arsenal acquitted themselves well, finishing in a respectable mid-table position. While they were not immediately among the top teams in the division, their performances demonstrated that they could compete at this level. The experience gained during this inaugural campaign was invaluable, providing the players and management with insights into what was required to succeed in the Football League.

The following season, 1894-95, saw Royal Arsenal continue to build on their foundation. The club began to develop a more consistent playing style, and their results improved accordingly. However, promotion to the First Division remained elusive, as the club faced stiff competition from more experienced teams.

During these early league campaigns, Royal Arsenal established themselves as a team to be reckoned with in the Second Division. The club's matches began to attract larger crowds, particularly for home games at the Manor Ground. The support from the local community was growing, and the club's profile was rising both locally and nationally.

These formative years in the Football League were crucial in shaping the future of the club. While Royal Arsenal did not achieve immediate success in terms of promotions or titles, they laid the groundwork for what was to come. The experience gained during these seasons, both on and off the pitch, would prove essential as the club continued to evolve.

Chapter 4: Woolwich Arsenal and Financial Struggles (1893-1904)

The Woolwich Years: The Club's Identity During Its Time in South London

As Royal Arsenal settled into life in the Football League, the club's identity began to evolve. By this time, the club was widely known as Woolwich Arsenal, reflecting its roots in the Royal Arsenal munitions factory and its location in Woolwich, South London. The name "Woolwich Arsenal" became synonymous with a hardworking, industrious team that mirrored the character of its supporters—many of whom were still workers from the factory.

The club's location in Woolwich was both a blessing and a curse. On one hand, it provided a loyal fan base drawn from the local community, who were passionate about their team. On the other hand, Woolwich's geographical position posed challenges, particularly in attracting players and supporters from outside the area. South London was not yet a footballing hotbed, and the club often struggled to draw the same level of attention and resources as clubs from the more affluent areas of London and the North.

Despite these challenges, Woolwich Arsenal developed a strong sense of identity. The club became known for its gritty, determined style of play, which resonated with the working-class supporters who filled the stands at the Manor Ground. The team's red shirts, adopted from their early days as Dial Square, became a symbol of their fighting spirit.

The Woolwich years were also a time of transition for the club. As football grew in popularity across England, Woolwich Arsenal found itself at the crossroads of maintaining its local identity while striving to compete on a national level. This period would test the club's resilience and determination, as they faced both on-field and off-field challenges.

Economic Challenges: Financial Difficulties and the Threat of Extinction

The early years in the Football League were marked by significant financial difficulties for Woolwich Arsenal. Running a professional football club was an expensive undertaking, and the costs associated with player wages, travel, and maintaining a home ground quickly added up. Despite the growing support from the local community, the club struggled to generate enough revenue to cover these expenses.

The financial strain was exacerbated by the club's location in Woolwich, which, while supportive, did not provide the same financial opportunities as clubs based in more central or affluent areas. The limited attendance at matches and the lack of wealthy backers meant that Woolwich Arsenal operated on a tight budget, often having to make difficult decisions to keep the club afloat.

During this period, the club faced the very real threat of extinction. There were times when it seemed that Woolwich Arsenal might not survive, as debts mounted and the financial pressures became overwhelming. The club's management worked tirelessly to find solutions, including exploring various fundraising efforts and seeking out potential investors. However, these efforts were often met with limited success, and the club's future remained uncertain.

One of the key figures during this challenging time was George Leavey, a local businessman who became heavily involved in the club's management. Leavey's financial support and business acumen were instrumental in keeping the club going during its darkest days. His commitment to Woolwich Arsenal helped to stabilize the club, even as it continued to struggle financially.

Despite the constant financial pressure, the club managed to persevere. Woolwich Arsenal's survival during this period was a testament to the dedication of its players, management, and supporters. They refused to give up, even when the odds seemed stacked against them, and this resilience would become a defining characteristic of the club.

First Highbury Connections: Early Discussions of Moving the Club

As Woolwich Arsenal continued to struggle financially, discussions began to emerge about the possibility of moving the club to a more lucrative location. The idea of relocating the club was controversial, as it meant leaving behind the community that had supported it since its inception. However, the financial realities of the situation made it clear that drastic action might be necessary to secure the club's future.

The first serious discussions about moving the club to North London began in the early 1900s. The club's management recognized that a move closer to the city center could provide access to a larger and wealthier fan base, as well as better facilities and financial backing. Highbury, a district in North London, emerged as a potential new home for the club.

The prospect of moving to Highbury was both exciting and daunting. On one hand, it offered the potential for growth and financial stability. On the other hand, it meant leaving behind the club's roots in Woolwich, which was an emotional and difficult decision for many involved with the club.

The early discussions about moving to Highbury were just the beginning of what would become a pivotal moment in the club's history. While the move would not be finalized until later, the seeds of change were being planted during this period. The club's management understood that to survive and thrive, Woolwich Arsenal might need to embrace a new identity and a new home.

These years of financial struggle and the consideration of relocation were a turning point for Woolwich Arsenal. The decisions made during this period would have lasting implications, shaping the future of the club and setting the stage for its transformation into one of England's most iconic football teams. Despite the hardships, Woolwich Arsenal's determination to survive and succeed remained unshaken, and this resilience would ultimately guide them through one of the most challenging periods in their history.

Chapter 5: The Move to Highbury (1904-1913)

Relocation to North London: The Decision and Logistics of Moving to Highbury

By the early 1900s, it had become increasingly clear that Woolwich Arsenal's future in South London was untenable. Despite the club's efforts to stabilize its finances, the challenges of maintaining a professional football club in Woolwich—an area with limited financial resources and a small local fanbase—were too great to ignore. The club's survival depended on bold action, and the idea of relocating to a more advantageous location began to gain traction among the club's management.

The decision to move the club to North London was not made lightly. It involved extensive discussions and planning, as well as significant logistical challenges. The primary motivation for the move was financial. North London, particularly the area around Highbury, offered access to a larger, more affluent population, which would not only increase matchday attendances but also attract potential investors and sponsors.

Finding a suitable site for the new stadium was a critical first step. Highbury, located in the London Borough of Islington, emerged as the ideal location. The area was well-connected by public transport, making it accessible to fans from across London. Additionally, Highbury had a relatively large, undeveloped area that could be transformed into a modern football stadium.

The logistics of the move were complex. The club had to secure the land, obtain planning permission, and raise the funds necessary to construct the new stadium. This process required negotiations with local authorities, potential investors, and other stakeholders. It also involved managing the expectations and emotions of the club's existing fanbase in Woolwich, many of whom were understandably upset by the prospect of losing their local team.

In 1913, after years of planning and negotiation, Woolwich Arsenal officially relocated to Highbury. The move marked a significant turning point in the club's history. It was a bold and controversial decision, but one that was ultimately driven by the need to secure the club's long-term future. The new stadium at Highbury was a state-of-the-art facility for its time, providing the club with the infrastructure it needed to compete at the highest level.

Sir Henry Norris: The Influential Role of Norris in the Move

The move to Highbury would not have been possible without the leadership and vision of Sir Henry Norris, one of the most influential figures in Arsenal's history. A businessman and politician, Norris had become involved with Woolwich Arsenal in the early 1910s, recognizing both the club's potential and its dire financial situation.

Norris was a pragmatic and ambitious man. He understood that for Woolwich Arsenal to survive and thrive, it needed to move to a location that offered greater financial opportunities. When the idea of relocating the club to North London was proposed, Norris became its most ardent supporter. He played a central role in securing the land at Highbury, negotiating the terms of the deal, and ensuring that the project was financially viable.

One of Norris's most significant contributions was his ability to secure funding for the move. He leveraged his connections in the business world to attract investors and sponsors, who were crucial in financing the construction of the new stadium. Norris also worked tirelessly to overcome the legal and logistical hurdles associated with the relocation, demonstrating his commitment to the club's future.

Norris's leadership extended beyond the practical aspects of the move. He was also instrumental in managing the public relations challenges that accompanied the relocation. Many fans and local residents in Woolwich were unhappy about the move, feeling that they were losing their beloved team. Norris understood the importance of maintaining the club's identity and worked to ensure that, despite the move, Arsenal remained connected to its roots in Woolwich.

Under Norris's guidance, the move to Highbury was successfully completed, and the club was rebranded as simply "Arsenal" to reflect its new identity. Norris's vision and determination were key factors in this transformation, and his influence would continue to shape the club in the years to come.

Settling In: The Early Years at Highbury and Their Impact on the Club's Identity

The move to Highbury marked the beginning of a new chapter in Arsenal's history. The club's first season at its new home, the 1913-14 campaign, was a period of adjustment. The team had to acclimate to its new surroundings, while the club's management worked to establish Arsenal as a major presence in North London.

The new stadium at Highbury was a source of pride for the club and its supporters. It was a modern facility, with a capacity of around 20,000, which could be expanded as needed. The stadium featured covered stands, offering protection from the elements, and was designed with the fan experience in mind. For the first time, Arsenal had a home that matched its ambitions.

The early years at Highbury were not without challenges. On the pitch, the team struggled initially, finding it difficult to achieve consistent results. However, the move to Highbury began to pay off as the club attracted larger crowds and increased revenue from ticket sales. The club's financial situation improved, allowing for greater investment in players and infrastructure.

The relocation to Highbury also had a profound impact on Arsenal's identity. The move marked the end of the club's association with Woolwich and its transformation into a more cosmopolitan, city-based club. The rebranding of the club as simply "Arsenal" reflected this shift, emphasizing its ambition to become one of the leading clubs in London and the country.

Highbury quickly became synonymous with Arsenal, and the stadium itself became a symbol of the club's new era. The move allowed Arsenal to attract a broader fanbase, including supporters from across London and beyond. This expansion of the club's support was crucial in establishing Arsenal as one of the most prominent and influential clubs in English football.

The early years at Highbury laid the foundation for Arsenal's future success. The move, guided by the vision of Sir Henry Norris, was a turning point that set the club on a path to becoming one of the giants of English football. While the transition was challenging, it ultimately proved to be a wise decision, as Arsenal began to realize its potential both on and off the pitch.

In the years that followed, Highbury would witness some of the most significant moments in Arsenal's history, becoming a hallowed ground for the club and its supporters. The move to Highbury was not just a change of location; it was the beginning of a new era, one that would see Arsenal rise to the heights of English football and become a club with a truly global identity.

Chapter 6: World War I and Its Impact (1914-1919)

The War Years: How World War I Affected the Club and Its Players

The outbreak of World War I in August 1914 brought an abrupt and profound disruption to football in England, and Arsenal was no exception. As the conflict escalated, the country's focus shifted from sport to the war effort, and football, like many other activities, was forced to take a backseat. The Football League decided to suspend official competitions at the end of the 1914-15 season, as thousands of young men, including many footballers, enlisted to serve their country.

For Arsenal, the war had an immediate and significant impact. Many of the club's players, staff, and supporters joined the armed forces. Footballers, who were often seen as symbols of physical fitness and patriotism, were encouraged to enlist, and many did so out of a sense of duty. Arsenal's squad, like those of other clubs, was depleted as its players went off to fight on the front lines.

The war also affected Arsenal's day-to-day operations. The Highbury stadium, which had only recently become the club's home, was repurposed for the war effort. The stadium and its facilities were used for military purposes, including training and storage, which meant that football was largely sidelined. Although some matches continued in the form of regional competitions and friendlies, these were often played with makeshift teams composed of remaining players and guest appearances from those on leave from the front.

The financial strain on the club during the war years was considerable. With official competitions suspended, matchday revenues all but disappeared. The club had to rely on the goodwill of its supporters and benefactors to stay afloat. Sir Henry Norris, who had played a crucial role in the club's move to Highbury, remained a key figure during this period, helping to ensure that Arsenal weathered the financial storm.

The human cost of the war was devastating. Several Arsenal players and former players lost their lives in the conflict, while others returned home with injuries that ended their football careers. The war took a heavy toll on the club, not just in terms of lost talent, but also in the emotional impact on the Arsenal community. The bonds between the club, its players, and its supporters were deepened by the shared experience of loss and sacrifice.

Post-War Recovery: The Immediate Post-War Challenges and Restructuring

When the war finally ended in November 1918, England was left to pick up the pieces, and the world of football was no different. Arsenal, like other clubs, faced the daunting task of rebuilding in the post-war period. The Football League was set to resume in the 1919-20 season, but there were significant challenges to overcome before normalcy could return.

One of the first tasks for Arsenal was to rebuild its squad. Many players who had served in the war were no longer able to play, either due to injury or the simple passage of time. The club needed to recruit new talent to replace those who had been lost. This was no easy task, as other clubs were also looking to strengthen their squads, leading to fierce competition for players.

Financial recovery was another pressing concern. The war had left Arsenal in a precarious financial position, with depleted resources and significant debts. The club's leadership, particularly Sir Henry Norris, worked tirelessly to stabilize the finances. This involved negotiating with creditors, securing new investments, and managing the day-to-day expenses of running the club in a period of economic uncertainty.

Highbury itself needed attention. During the war, the stadium had been repurposed for military use, and it required refurbishment and maintenance to be ready for the return of league football. The club invested in necessary repairs and improvements to ensure that the stadium could once again serve as a proper home for Arsenal.

The social and psychological impact of the war on both players and supporters also needed to be addressed. The Arsenal community, like the rest of the country, had been deeply affected by the war's horrors. The return of football provided a sense of normalcy and a means of healing, but it was clear that things would never be the same as they were before 1914.

The immediate post-war years were marked by a sense of determination and resilience. Arsenal, like the nation itself, was committed to moving forward despite the challenges. The club's ability to navigate this difficult period set the stage for its future successes and established a foundation of strength and solidarity that would define Arsenal in the years to come.

Chapter 7: The Controversial Promotion (1919)

Election to the First Division: The Controversial Circumstances of Arsenal's Promotion

As football resumed after the war, the Football League underwent a significant reorganization. One of the key changes was the expansion of the First Division from 20 to 22 teams. This expansion created two additional spots in the top flight, which would be filled by clubs elected by the league's existing members. The process of election, however, would become one of the most controversial moments in Arsenal's history.

At the end of the 1914-15 season, Arsenal had finished fifth in the Second Division, which under normal circumstances would not have been sufficient for promotion. However, the post-war restructuring offered an unexpected opportunity. Sir Henry Norris, who had become increasingly influential within the Football League, saw this as a chance to elevate Arsenal to the First Division, where he believed the club rightfully belonged given its potential and ambition.

Norris embarked on a campaign to secure Arsenal's election to the top tier. He leveraged his connections within the league and argued that Arsenal's move to Highbury, its solid infrastructure, and its potential to draw large crowds in North London made it a deserving candidate for promotion. This campaign was successful, and Arsenal was controversially elected to the First Division at the expense of clubs like Tottenham Hotspur, who were one of Arsenal's local rivals and had finished higher in the Second Division during the last completed season.

The decision sparked outrage and accusations of unfair play, particularly from Tottenham, who felt that they had been unfairly passed over. Rumors of backroom deals and undue influence swirled around the election, though no concrete evidence of wrongdoing was ever produced. Nevertheless, the promotion solidified Arsenal's place in the First Division, where they would remain for decades to come.

This controversial promotion marked a significant turning point in Arsenal's history. It not only secured the club's future in the top flight but also intensified the rivalry with Tottenham, which would become one of the fiercest in English football. The episode also demonstrated the growing influence of Sir Henry Norris, whose actions, though controversial, were crucial in positioning Arsenal as a major force in English football.

Building a Competitive Squad: Early Efforts to Establish a Top-Tier Team

With Arsenal now in the First Division, the club faced the immediate challenge of building a squad capable of competing at the highest level. The post-war years had left the team depleted, and the quality of players needed to be significantly improved to ensure survival in the top flight.

Arsenal's recruitment strategy focused on attracting experienced players who could provide the stability and leadership needed during this transitional period. The club also sought to develop younger talent, aiming to create a balance between seasoned professionals and emerging prospects. This approach was essential for building a team that could not only compete in the First Division but also establish Arsenal as a credible force in English football.

Key signings during this period included players with proven track records in the First Division, as well as promising talents from lower leagues. The club's management, under the guidance of Sir Henry Norris, worked diligently to identify and secure these players, often outmaneuvering rival clubs in the process.

The squad-building efforts were not without challenges. Financial constraints remained a concern, and the club had to be strategic in its spending. Nevertheless, Arsenal managed to assemble a team that was competitive, if not immediately among the elite. The emphasis on discipline, teamwork, and tactical acumen became hallmarks of Arsenal's playing style during these early years in the First Division.

The club's early performances in the top flight were mixed, reflecting the growing pains of a team adapting to a higher level of competition. However, there were signs of progress, and the foundations were being laid for future success. Arsenal's presence in the First Division also helped to attract larger crowds to Highbury, increasing the club's revenue and enabling further investment in the squad.

Rivalries and Relationships: Arsenal's Growing Presence in the First Division

Arsenal's entry into the First Division not only changed the club's competitive landscape but also intensified its relationships with other clubs, particularly in London. The most significant of these was the rivalry with Tottenham Hotspur, which was exacerbated by the controversial circumstances of Arsenal's promotion. The rivalry, often referred to as the North London Derby, quickly became one of the most passionate and hotly contested in English football.

Matches between Arsenal and Tottenham were fiercely competitive, both on and off the pitch. For Tottenham, Arsenal's promotion was seen as an injustice, and this added a layer of intensity to their encounters. For Arsenal, establishing dominance over their local rivals became a point of pride and a crucial part of their identity in the First Division.

Beyond Tottenham, Arsenal also began to develop rivalries with other top-tier clubs, including Chelsea, West Ham United, and the traditional powerhouses of the North such as Manchester United and Liverpool. These rivalries were born out of the natural competition in the league, as Arsenal sought to establish itself as a serious contender for honors.

The relationships between Arsenal and other clubs during this period were also shaped by the broader dynamics of English football. The post-war era was one of rebuilding and growth, with clubs across the country striving to regain their pre-war status or establish new legacies. Arsenal's ambitions and the aggressive approach taken by Sir Henry Norris sometimes put the club at odds with others, but it also earned them respect as a club determined to succeed.

Arsenal's growing presence in the First Division was not just about on-field performance; it was also about establishing a reputation as a club that belonged among the elite. The early years were challenging, but they were also crucial in laying the groundwork for Arsenal's evolution into one of the most successful and influential clubs in English football.

Chapter 8: The Chapman Revolution Begins (1925-1930)

Herbert Chapman's Arrival: His Appointment and Early Changes

The summer of 1925 marked a turning point in Arsenal's history with the appointment of Herbert Chapman as the club's new manager. Arsenal had struggled to find consistent success in the years following World War I, and the club's leadership recognized the need for a visionary figure to take the team to new heights. Chapman, who had already made a name for himself by leading Huddersfield Town to consecutive league titles, was seen as the perfect candidate to revolutionize Arsenal.

Chapman's arrival was not just a managerial change; it was the beginning of a complete overhaul of the club's approach to football. From the moment he stepped into Highbury, Chapman exuded confidence and ambition. He brought with him a wealth of experience, a deep understanding of the game, and a forward-thinking philosophy that would soon set Arsenal apart from their rivals.

One of Chapman's first actions was to modernize the club's infrastructure. He insisted on improving training facilities, implementing more rigorous fitness regimes, and bringing in specialized coaching staff. Chapman believed that success on the pitch began with meticulous preparation off it, and he wasted no time in laying the foundations for what would become a footballing dynasty.

Chapman also recognized the importance of a strong backroom team. He brought in key figures such as Tom Whittaker, who would later become a legendary Arsenal manager in his own right, and George Allison, who was instrumental in the club's media and public relations efforts. Together, they began to shape a new identity for Arsenal, one that was based on professionalism, innovation, and a relentless pursuit of excellence.

Tactical Innovations: The Introduction of the WM Formation

Perhaps the most significant contribution Chapman made to Arsenal and football in general was his tactical innovation. During the 1925-26 season, the Football Association changed the offside rule, reducing the number of opposing players required to be between the attacking player and the goal from three to two. This change had a profound impact on the game, leading to an increase in goals and a need for new defensive strategies.

Chapman, ever the tactician, responded by developing the famous WM formation, a revolutionary approach that would redefine football tactics. The WM formation, named for the shape it formed on the pitch, was a 3-2-2-3 system that provided greater defensive solidity while maintaining attacking potency. The formation featured three defenders at the back, two half-backs shielding them, two inside forwards in midfield, and three forwards leading the attack.

This system allowed Arsenal to strike a balance between defense and attack, giving them the ability to quickly transition from one to the other. The three defenders provided a solid backbone, while the wing-halves offered both defensive support and attacking width. The inside forwards and the center forward formed a dynamic attacking trio, capable of breaking down opposition defenses with pace and precision.

The introduction of the WM formation not only transformed Arsenal's fortunes on the pitch but also had a lasting impact on the game as a whole. Other clubs soon began to adopt similar systems, and the WM formation became a standard in English football for decades. Chapman's tactical genius set Arsenal on a path to success and established him as one of the most influential figures in the history of the sport.

Building a Dynasty: Key Signings and the Foundations for Future Success

With the tactical foundation in place, Chapman set about building a team capable of executing his vision. He was a master at identifying talent, and his ability to spot players who could thrive in his system was key to Arsenal's success. Chapman's transfer dealings during this period were shrewd and strategic, focusing on bringing in players who possessed both skill and intelligence.

One of Chapman's most important signings was the Scottish inside forward Alex James, who joined Arsenal from Preston North End in 1929. James was the creative fulcrum of Chapman's team, a player with exceptional vision, passing ability, and footballing intelligence. His role in the WM formation was crucial, as he linked midfield and attack, dictating the tempo of the game and providing the spark that Arsenal needed to unlock opposition defenses.

Another key signing was Cliff Bastin, a young winger who joined Arsenal in 1929 from Exeter City. Bastin quickly became one of the most prolific forwards in English football, his speed and finishing ability making him a perfect fit for Chapman's system. At just 17 years old, Bastin was a revelation, and his goalscoring prowess would become a hallmark of Arsenal's success in the years to come.

Chapman also reinforced the defense, bringing in players like Eddie Hapgood and George Male, who would become stalwarts of Arsenal's backline. Hapgood, in particular, was a commanding presence at left-back, known for his leadership and defensive acumen. Under Chapman's guidance, these players developed into a cohesive and formidable unit, capable of competing at the highest level.

Beyond the individual signings, Chapman's broader vision was to create a team that embodied Arsenal's values of discipline, professionalism, and innovation. He instilled a winning mentality within the squad, emphasizing the importance of teamwork and tactical intelligence. The foundations laid during this period would not only lead to immediate success but also set the stage for Arsenal's dominance in the 1930s and beyond.

Chapter 9: The First Taste of Glory (1930-1933)

The 1930 FA Cup Victory: Arsenal's First Major Trophy Under Chapman

The 1929-30 season marked a turning point for Arsenal as they secured their first major trophy under Herbert Chapman's leadership. The FA Cup was the most prestigious domestic competition in England at the time, and Arsenal's journey to the final was a testament to the progress they had made under Chapman's guidance.

Arsenal reached the FA Cup final in 1930, where they faced Huddersfield Town, Chapman's former club. The final, held at Wembley Stadium, was a highly anticipated event, with over 92,000 spectators in attendance. The match was also notable for being the first to feature the iconic "Community Singing" before the game, a tradition that has continued to this day.

Arsenal took the lead through Alex James, who scored a brilliant solo goal, dribbling past several Huddersfield defenders before calmly slotting the ball into the net. James's goal was a moment of magic that showcased his exceptional talent and justified Chapman's decision to make him the centerpiece of the team.

The second goal came late in the game, with Jack Lambert securing the victory for Arsenal. Lambert, who had been one of Chapman's key signings, finished off a well-worked move to make it 2-0. The final whistle sparked jubilant scenes among the Arsenal players and supporters, as the club celebrated its first-ever FA Cup triumph.

The 1930 FA Cup victory was a watershed moment for Arsenal. It was the club's first major trophy, and it provided tangible proof that Chapman's methods were working. The victory also marked the beginning of a golden era for Arsenal, as they established themselves as one of the dominant forces in English football.

League Title Success: Winning the League in 1931 and 1933

Buoyed by their FA Cup success, Arsenal entered the 1930-31 season with renewed confidence and ambition. Chapman's team had matured into a formidable outfit, and they embarked on a campaign that would see them crowned champions of England for the first time in the club's history.

Arsenal's league campaign was characterized by a combination of tactical brilliance, individual flair, and collective determination. The WM formation, which had been honed to perfection, allowed

Arsenal to dominate matches both defensively and offensively. The team's attacking trio of Alex James, Cliff Bastin, and David Jack wreaked havoc on opposition defenses, while the defense, marshaled by Eddie Hapgood, was resolute and disciplined.

Arsenal secured the league title with an impressive 66 points, five points clear of their nearest rivals, Aston Villa. The title win was a culmination of years of hard work and careful planning under Chapman's leadership. It was also a vindication of Chapman's innovative approach to the game, as Arsenal's success was built on the tactical foundations he had laid.

The 1931 title was followed by another in 1933, as Arsenal continued to assert their dominance in English football. The 1932-33 season saw Arsenal once again finish as champions, this time with a remarkable 58 points. The consistency of Arsenal's performances during this period was a testament to the strength and depth of the squad that Chapman had assembled.

These league titles cemented Arsenal's place among the elite clubs in England. Chapman's vision of creating a dynasty was becoming a reality, as Arsenal's success on the pitch translated into increased support off it. Highbury became a fortress, with crowds flocking to see the team that had revolutionized English football.

Star Players: Profiles of Chapman's Key Players, Including Alex James and Cliff Bastin

Herbert Chapman's Arsenal was built around a core of exceptional players, each of whom played a crucial role in the team's success. Among them, Alex James and Cliff Bastin stood out as two of the most influential figures in the club's history.

Alex James was the creative heartbeat of Chapman's Arsenal. Born in Mossend, Scotland, James began his career at Raith Rovers before moving to Preston North End, where he caught the eye of Chapman. In 1929, James joined Arsenal for a then-substantial fee of £8,750, a move that would prove to be one of the most important in the club's history.

James was a playmaker in the truest sense of the word. His vision, passing ability, and footballing intelligence were unmatched, and he was capable of unlocking even the most stubborn defenses with a single pass. James's role in the WM formation was to operate as the link between midfield and attack, dictating the flow of the game and providing the creative spark that Arsenal needed to break down opposition teams.

Despite his slight build and unassuming demeanor, James was a fierce competitor who relished the big occasions. His performances in key matches, including the 1930 FA Cup final, were instrumental in Arsenal's success during this period. James's influence on the pitch extended beyond his technical abilities; he was a leader who commanded respect from his teammates and opponents alike.

Cliff Bastin was another key figure in Chapman's Arsenal. Born in Exeter, Bastin joined Arsenal in 1929 at the age of 17, having already made a name for himself as a prodigious talent at Exeter City. Bastin was a winger with blistering pace, a powerful shot, and an uncanny ability to find the back of the net.

Bastin's goalscoring record for Arsenal was remarkable. He was the club's top scorer in several seasons during the 1930s, and his partnership with Alex James was one of the most effective in English football. Bastin's ability to cut inside from the wing and score goals made him a constant threat to opposition defenses, and he quickly became a fan favorite at Highbury.

Bastin's impact on Arsenal was not limited to his goalscoring prowess. He was also a tireless worker who embodied the values of discipline and teamwork that Chapman instilled in the squad.

Bastin's contributions were integral to Arsenal's league titles in 1931 and 1933, and his legacy as one of the club's greatest players endures to this day.

Under Chapman's guidance, players like James and Bastin flourished, and together they helped to establish Arsenal as the dominant force in English football during the early 1930s. The foundations laid by Chapman and his players during this period would have a lasting impact, shaping the future of Arsenal and setting the standard for success at the club for generations to come.

Chapter 10: The Sudden Loss of Chapman (1934)

Chapman's Untimely Death: The Impact on the Club and Football World

On January 6, 1934, Arsenal and the wider football world were shocked by the sudden death of Herbert Chapman, who passed away from pneumonia at the age of 55. Chapman's death was not just a loss for Arsenal; it was a monumental loss for football as a whole. He had been a transformative figure, not only in terms of his success on the pitch but also for his innovations and forward-thinking approach to the game.

Chapman's influence extended far beyond tactical formations and player management. He had introduced floodlights for training, advocated for numbered shirts, and even pushed for the use of white footballs to make the game easier to follow for spectators. His vision for the sport was broad and ambitious, and he was constantly seeking ways to improve both the game and the experience for fans.

The news of Chapman's death sent ripples throughout the football community. Players, managers, and supporters alike mourned the loss of a man who had come to symbolize the modern game. At Arsenal, his passing left a void that seemed impossible to fill. The club had been riding high under his leadership, having secured multiple league titles and an FA Cup, and his death raised questions about how the team would continue without the man who had been its driving force.

For the players, many of whom had been personally selected and nurtured by Chapman, his death was a deeply personal loss. The bond between Chapman and his squad was strong, built on mutual respect and a shared commitment to excellence. The shock of his passing threatened to destabilize the team at a time when they were at the peak of their powers.

However, Chapman's influence had been so profound that his philosophy and methods had become deeply ingrained in the club's culture. This provided a foundation for Arsenal to continue its success, even in the absence of the man who had led them to greatness.

Continuing Success Under George Allison: Maintaining the Momentum Post-Chapman

Following Chapman's death, the responsibility of leading Arsenal fell to Joe Shaw, the club's reserve team coach, who took over on an interim basis. Shaw was well-versed in Chapman's methods and ensured that the team maintained its focus during this difficult time. Under his temporary stewardship,

Arsenal continued their campaign and managed to keep pace at the top of the league.

In the summer of 1934, George Allison, a close associate of Chapman and the club's former press officer, was appointed as the new manager. Allison was not a traditional football manager in the sense of being a former player or coach, but he had a deep understanding of the game and a strong connection with the club. His background in journalism and public relations also meant he was adept at handling the pressures of managing a top team.

Allison's primary task was to maintain the momentum that Chapman had built. He wisely chose not to make drastic changes to the team or its style of play, instead continuing with the strategies and tactics that had brought so much success under Chapman. This continuity was crucial in ensuring that Arsenal remained a dominant force in English football.

Allison also had the benefit of inheriting a squad that was already brimming with talent and confidence. Players like Alex James, Cliff Bastin, and Eddie Hapgood were at the peak of their powers, and they responded positively to Allison's leadership. The team's unity and shared sense of purpose, fostered under Chapman, were critical in navigating the transition to new management.

Allison's approach proved successful. He managed to keep the team focused and motivated, guiding them through the remainder of the 1933-34 season. Arsenal, driven by a desire to honor Chapman's legacy, continued to perform at a high level, and their determination was rewarded with further success.

More Titles and Trophies: Further League Titles in 1934 and 1935

Despite the tragic loss of Herbert Chapman, Arsenal went on to win the First Division title at the end of the 1933-34 season. This triumph was a testament to the strength of the team that Chapman had built and the ability of George Allison to steer the club through turbulent times. The league victory was particularly poignant, as it served as a fitting tribute to Chapman's legacy and underscored the resilience of the club.

Arsenal's dominance continued into the 1934-35 season. With Allison at the helm, the team once again asserted its superiority in the league, clinching another First Division title. This period of success established Arsenal as the preeminent club in English football, with three league titles in a row—1933, 1934, and 1935—a remarkable achievement that cemented their status as the era's dominant force.

The 1934-35 season was notable for several standout performances. The attacking prowess of players like Cliff Bastin and Ted Drake was instrumental in Arsenal's success. Drake, in particular, made history during this season by scoring a record seven goals in a single match against Aston Villa, a feat that remains unmatched in top-flight English football.

Arsenal's ability to continue winning titles in the aftermath of Chapman's death demonstrated the depth of talent and the enduring quality of the squad he had assembled. It also highlighted the effectiveness of Allison's management, which was based on maintaining the principles and standards that Chapman had instilled.

The continued success of Arsenal during this period was a source of pride for the club and its supporters. It showed that the foundations laid by Chapman were strong enough to withstand even the most challenging of circumstances, and it reinforced Arsenal's reputation as a club capable of sustained excellence.

Chapter 11: The Road to War (1936-1939)

Last Pre-War Successes: The 1936 FA Cup Win and Subsequent League Performances

As Arsenal moved into the second half of the 1930s, the club continued to build on its earlier successes, with the 1935-36 season bringing yet another major trophy to Highbury. This time, it was the FA Cup, a competition that held a special place in English football and in the hearts of Arsenal supporters.

The 1936 FA Cup final saw Arsenal face Sheffield United at Wembley Stadium. The match was a tightly contested affair, with both teams showing strong defensive capabilities. However, it was Arsenal who managed to break the deadlock, thanks to a goal from Ted Drake, the prolific striker who had been a key figure in the team's success over the past few seasons. Drake's goal secured a 1-0 victory for Arsenal, giving the club its second FA Cup triumph.

This victory was significant for several reasons. Firstly, it reinforced Arsenal's status as one of the top teams in the country, capable of winning both league titles and cup competitions. Secondly, it provided further evidence of George Allison's ability to guide the club to success in the post-Chapman era. The win also brought joy to the

Arsenal faithful, who continued to support the team with unwavering enthusiasm.

Following the FA Cup victory, Arsenal's league performances remained strong, though they were unable to replicate the dominance of the early 1930s. The team consistently finished near the top of the table, but the intensity of competition and the gradual aging of some key players meant that further league titles proved elusive.

The latter half of the 1930s saw Arsenal begin to transition from the team that had dominated English football under Chapman. While the club was still highly competitive, the focus began to shift towards rebuilding and preparing for the future, particularly as the shadow of another global conflict began to loom over Europe.

Preparing for Conflict: How Arsenal Prepared for the Coming War

As the 1930s drew to a close, the political situation in Europe grew increasingly tense. The rise of Nazi Germany and the threat of war cast a long shadow over all aspects of life in Britain, including football. Arsenal, like other clubs, began to prepare for the possibility that the outbreak of war could once again disrupt the game.

The club's leadership, mindful of the experiences of World War I, started to make contingency plans for how to deal with the potential impact of another conflict. These plans included ensuring the financial stability of the club, maintaining the stadium and facilities at Highbury, and preparing for the loss of players to military service.

Many of Arsenal's players, like those across the country, were called up to serve in the armed forces as tensions escalated. This had a direct impact on the team's ability to compete, as key players were either conscripted or volunteered for service. The loss of these players meant that the club had to rely more on younger, less experienced players, as well as those who were not yet of military age.

Despite these challenges, Arsenal continued to compete in the Football League, albeit with the understanding that the situation could change at any moment. The club also played a role in supporting the war effort, with Highbury once again being repurposed for military use, as it had been during World War I. The stadium was used as an Air Raid Precautions (ARP) center, providing a base for civil defense operations.

The preparations for war were a sobering reminder of the uncertainty and danger that lay ahead. For Arsenal, it was a time of reflection and resilience, as the club sought to navigate the difficult circumstances while remaining true to the values and traditions that had been established over the previous decades.

Legacy of the 1930s Team: The Lasting Impact of the Pre-War Arsenal Teams

The Arsenal teams of the 1930s left an indelible mark on the history of the club and on English football as a whole. Under the leadership of Herbert Chapman, and later George Allison, Arsenal had established itself as the dominant force in English football, setting new standards for excellence both on and off the pitch.

The tactical innovations introduced by Chapman, particularly the WM formation, had revolutionized the way the game was played, influencing football tactics for generations. Arsenal's success during this period demonstrated the effectiveness of a well-organized, professional approach to football, and the club's achievements inspired other teams to adopt similar methods.

The players who formed the core of Arsenal's team in the 1930s—such as Alex James, Cliff Bastin, Eddie Hapgood, and Ted Drake—became legends in their own right. Their contributions to the club's success were immense, and their names would forever be associated with the golden era of Arsenal football. These players not only brought trophies to Highbury but also helped to forge the identity of Arsenal as a club that valued skill, intelligence, and teamwork.

The legacy of the 1930s team extended beyond their on-field achievements. They helped to elevate Arsenal to a position of prominence within English football, laying the foundations for the club's future successes. The spirit of innovation, professionalism, and ambition that characterized Arsenal during this period would continue to define the club in the years to come.

As the world moved closer to war, the Arsenal teams of the 1930s stood as a reminder of what could be achieved through vision, dedication, and unity. Their legacy would endure, providing inspiration and a standard of excellence for future generations of Arsenal players and supporters.

Chapter 12: The Immediate Post-War Period (1945-1950)

Return to Football: Resumption of the League After World War II

The conclusion of World War II in 1945 marked the beginning of a new chapter for Arsenal and the broader football community. As the nation began to rebuild, so too did the world of football, which had been on hold for the duration of the conflict. The Football League resumed in the 1946-47 season, and for Arsenal, the post-war period was both a time of renewal and of significant challenges.

The war had left its mark on Arsenal, as it had on all clubs. Highbury had been heavily damaged by bombing, with parts of the stadium destroyed or severely affected. The club faced the daunting task of repairing the ground and restoring it to its former glory. Despite the difficulties, the Arsenal management, led by Chairman Bracewell Smith and manager Tom Whittaker, was determined to return the club to the top of English football.

Player recruitment was another challenge. Many of the pre-war stars had either retired or were no longer the force they once were due to the effects of the war. Arsenal, like other clubs, had to rebuild its squad almost from scratch. The club turned to a mix of young, promising players and experienced veterans to form a competitive team.

The 1946-47 season was one of adjustment, as the team sought to find its rhythm in a league that had changed dramatically due to the long hiatus. Arsenal finished in mid-table, a respectable but unspectacular return to league football. However, the foundation was being laid for what would soon become a successful period in the club's history.

The 1947-48 League Title: Arsenal's First Post-War League Triumph

The 1947-48 season saw Arsenal reclaim their place at the summit of English football with a dominant performance that culminated in their first league title since before the war. Under the stewardship of Tom Whittaker, who had taken over as manager following the untimely death of George Allison, Arsenal displayed the kind of form that had made them the preeminent club in England during the 1930s.

Whittaker, who had been a close associate of Herbert Chapman, brought with him a deep understanding of the tactical innovations that had made Arsenal successful in the past. He combined this knowledge with his own managerial philosophy, emphasizing teamwork, discipline, and a strong defensive foundation.

The key to Arsenal's success in the 1947-48 season was their consistency and resilience. The team boasted a well-balanced squad with stars such as Joe Mercer, a commanding presence in midfield, and Ronnie Rooke, a prolific striker who finished as the league's top scorer. Arsenal's defense, marshaled by the experienced Leslie Compton and Laurie Scott, was among the best in the league, conceding just 32 goals in 42 matches.

Arsenal clinched the title with a total of 59 points, seven points clear of their nearest rivals, Manchester United. The championship was a testament to the club's ability to rebuild and adapt in the post-war era. It also reaffirmed Arsenal's status as one of the leading clubs in English football, capable of overcoming adversity and returning to the top of the league.

The 1947-48 title win was celebrated by Arsenal supporters as a significant achievement, not just because it marked the club's return to glory, but also because it symbolized the resilience and determination of the team and its management. For Whittaker, it was a personal triumph, as he had succeeded in leading Arsenal back to the pinnacle of English football in his first full season as manager.

FA Cup Victory: The 1950 FA Cup Win and Its Significance

Two years after their league triumph, Arsenal added another major trophy to their collection by winning the FA Cup in 1950. The victory was significant for several reasons, not least because it was the club's first FA Cup win since 1936 and only their third overall.

The 1949-50 FA Cup campaign saw Arsenal demonstrate their ability to perform in knockout football, with a series of strong performances that took them to the final at Wembley Stadium. The final, played on April 29, 1950, pitted Arsenal against Liverpool, a team that had emerged as a formidable force in post-war football.

In front of a crowd of over 100,000 spectators, Arsenal produced a composed and disciplined performance. The match was tightly contested, but Arsenal's experience and quality ultimately shone through. Reg Lewis, Arsenal's reliable forward, was the hero of the day, scoring both goals in a 2-0 victory that secured the trophy for the Gunners.

The 1950 FA Cup win was a source of immense pride for Arsenal. It reinforced the club's reputation as one of the most successful teams in English football and provided a tangible reward for the hard work and dedication of the players and management. For many of the squad, including Tom Whittaker, the victory was particularly sweet, as it capped off a period of rebuilding and marked Arsenal's return to the top tier of English football.

The significance of the FA Cup win extended beyond the trophy itself. It was a testament to the club's resilience in the face of the challenges posed by the post-war era, and it helped to solidify Arsenal's place in the hearts of their supporters. The triumph at Wembley was celebrated with great enthusiasm, both in London and across the country, as Arsenal once again demonstrated their ability to rise to the occasion on the biggest stage.

Chapter 13: A Declining Force (1951-1958)

Challenges in the 1950s: Arsenal's Struggle to Maintain Their Dominance

The early 1950s, while starting on a high note with Arsenal's FA Cup victory in 1950, soon became a period of increasing difficulty for the club. Maintaining the dominance that Arsenal had enjoyed in previous decades proved challenging, as the team struggled with aging players, injuries, and a shifting football landscape.

One of the primary challenges Arsenal faced during this period was the inability to consistently replace key players who had been instrumental in the club's success. The squad that had won the league in 1948 and the FA Cup in 1950 was beginning to show signs of wear. Many of the stars from those teams were nearing the end of their careers, and finding suitable replacements was not always straightforward.

Injuries also played a significant role in Arsenal's decline. The physical demands of post-war football, combined with the natural aging process, meant that several of Arsenal's key players were frequently sidelined. This inconsistency in team selection hindered Arsenal's ability to build momentum and challenge for titles on a regular basis.

Moreover, the overall level of competition in English football was rising. Other clubs were investing in their squads and facilities, and the tactical innovations that had once set Arsenal apart were now being adopted and adapted by rivals. Clubs like Wolverhampton Wanderers, Tottenham Hotspur, and particularly Manchester United were becoming major forces in the league, making it harder for Arsenal to maintain their position at the top.

As the 1950s progressed, Arsenal's performances in the league became increasingly erratic. The club fluctuated between mid-table finishes and occasional pushes for the top four, but the consistency that had characterized the Chapman and early post-war eras was missing. This period of decline was a source of frustration for supporters who had become accustomed to seeing their team regularly compete for honors.

Key Players and Management: Influential Figures During a Difficult Decade

Despite the challenges, there were still individuals within the club who made significant contributions during the 1950s. Tom Whittaker, who had led Arsenal to post-war success, remained a respected figure until his untimely death in 1956. Whittaker's tenure as manager, though increasingly difficult in his later years, was marked by his deep commitment to the club and his ability to keep Arsenal competitive in a rapidly changing football environment.

After Whittaker's death, Jack Crayston briefly took over as manager, followed by George Swindin, who was appointed in 1958. Both managers faced the daunting task of rebuilding an aging squad while trying to restore Arsenal to its former glory. However, their tenures were marked by inconsistency, and neither could replicate the success that Arsenal had enjoyed in previous decades.

On the pitch, players like Jimmy Logie and Doug Lishman continued to perform admirably, providing moments of brilliance even as the team struggled as a whole. Logie, a creative midfielder, was one of the last links to the great Arsenal teams of the late 1940s, and his influence remained vital during the early 1950s. Lishman, a forward with a keen eye for goal, was a consistent scorer for Arsenal, helping to keep the team competitive in the league.

Defensively, players like Joe Mercer and Ray Daniel were key figures. Mercer, who had captained Arsenal to the 1948 league title, remained a respected leader on the field, while Daniel provided stability at the back. However, as the decade wore on, it became clear that Arsenal needed fresh talent to revitalize the squad.

The Rise of Rivals: The Emergence of Manchester United and Other Competitors

During the 1950s, Arsenal's decline coincided with the rise of several rival clubs that would go on to challenge the Gunners' position in English football. Among these, Manchester United, under the management of Matt Busby, emerged as the most formidable opponent.

Busby's United team, known as the "Busby Babes" due to the youth of many of its star players, captured the imagination of football fans with their dynamic style of play and attacking prowess. Players like Duncan Edwards, Bobby Charlton, and Tommy Taylor became household names, and Manchester United quickly established themselves as the dominant force in English football during the late 1950s.

Arsenal's struggles were further compounded by the success of other clubs, including Wolverhampton Wanderers, who under Stan Cullis became one of the most successful teams in the country, and Tottenham Hotspur, Arsenal's fierce North London rivals, who were building a team that would soon challenge for top honors.

These developments highlighted the changing landscape of English football. The post-war years had seen a shift in power, with new clubs rising to prominence and others, like Arsenal, facing the challenge of maintaining their status. The 1950s were a time of transition, and for Arsenal, it was a period of reflection and reevaluation as the club sought to find a way back to the top.

Chapter 14: Searching for Stability (1958-1966)

Billy Wright's Era: The Challenges and Reforms Under Manager Billy Wright

In 1958, Arsenal appointed Billy Wright as manager in an effort to reverse the club's declining fortunes. Wright, a legendary figure in English football and a former captain of the national team, was seen as a high-profile choice who could bring leadership and discipline to Arsenal's underperforming squad.

Wright's appointment was met with optimism, as his reputation as a player suggested he had the qualities needed to succeed in management. However, his transition from player to manager proved challenging. Wright inherited a team that was in need of significant overhaul, both in terms of personnel and tactics, and his lack of managerial experience soon became apparent.

One of Wright's primary objectives was to modernize the club. He introduced new training methods, sought to improve the club's scouting network, and focused on developing younger players who could form the core of the team in the future. Wright was also keen to instill a sense of discipline within the squad, emphasizing the importance of professionalism and dedication.

Despite these efforts, Wright struggled to achieve consistent results. The team's performances in the league remained erratic, and the squad often lacked the cohesion and tactical awareness needed to compete with the top clubs. Wright's attempts to implement new ideas were often met with resistance from players who were used to the methods of previous managers, and this friction contributed to the difficulties Arsenal faced during his tenure.

The Modernization Effort: Attempts to Modernize the Club and Its Facilities

During Billy Wright's time as manager, there was a recognition that Arsenal needed to modernize not just on the pitch, but off it as well. The club's facilities at Highbury, while iconic, were beginning to show their age, and there was a growing need to bring the club into the modern era.

Wright, along with the club's board, pushed for improvements to the training facilities and the stadium itself. The aim was to create an environment that would attract top players and help develop the talent already at the club. Investments were made in upgrading the training ground and improving the medical facilities, reflecting the increasing importance of sports science in football.

The club also began to focus more on youth development, recognizing that the future of Arsenal depended on cultivating homegrown talent. This period saw the beginnings of a more structured youth academy, which would later become one of the pillars of Arsenal's success in the years to come.

However, these modernization efforts were not without their challenges. Financial constraints limited the extent of the improvements that could be made, and the club often found itself playing catch-up with other teams that had been quicker to adapt to the changing demands of modern football.

Mixed Results: The Fluctuating Fortunes of Arsenal in the Early 1960s

The early 1960s were a period of mixed fortunes for Arsenal. Under Billy Wright, the team showed flashes of potential, but consistency remained elusive. The league performances were characterized by mid-table finishes, far from the glory days of the 1930s and late 1940s. Wright's tenure saw Arsenal finish as low as 13th in the 1962-63 season, a stark reminder of how far the club had fallen from its previous heights.

There were moments of promise, such as a strong run in the 1961-62 season that saw Arsenal briefly challenge for the top spots before fading towards the end of the campaign. However, these moments were too infrequent to suggest that Arsenal was on the path back to success.

The club's struggles were compounded by the emergence of Tottenham Hotspur as a major force in English football. Spurs' double-winning season in 1960-61, where they claimed both the league title and the FA Cup, only served to highlight Arsenal's decline. The North London rivalry, always intense, took on new significance as Spurs enjoyed success while Arsenal languished in mid-table.

The fluctuating fortunes of Arsenal during this period reflected the broader challenges the club faced. Wright's efforts to modernize and reform the team were noble, but the results on the pitch did not match the ambition. By the mid-1960s, it was clear that further changes were needed if Arsenal were to return to the upper echelons of English football.

Wright's tenure ultimately came to an end in 1966, marking the conclusion of a difficult era for the club. While he had brought professionalism and a desire for modernization to Arsenal, the results had not lived up to expectations. The search for stability continued, and the club now faced the task of finding a new direction that could lead them back to success.

Chapter 15: The Bertie Mee Era Begins (1966-1970)

Mee's Appointment: The Background and Strategy of Bertie Mee

In 1966, Arsenal was at a crossroads. The club had endured a difficult decade, struggling to recapture the glory of earlier years. The board knew they needed a fresh approach, and the appointment of Bertie Mee as manager was a bold, if unconventional, choice. Mee, who had been Arsenal's physiotherapist since 1960, had no prior managerial experience, yet his understanding of the players, combined with his meticulous approach to the game, convinced the board that he was the right man to lead the club into a new era.

Mee's background as a physiotherapist brought a unique perspective to his management style. He was deeply familiar with the physical demands of the game and had a strong rapport with the players, having worked closely with them on their fitness and recovery. Mee's appointment was initially viewed with skepticism by some, but he quickly set about proving his doubters wrong.

One of Mee's key strategies was to focus on discipline, organization, and fitness. He believed that a well-drilled, physically strong team could compete with the best, even if they lacked the star power of other sides. Mee also understood the importance of building a cohesive unit and placed great emphasis on teamwork, both on and off the pitch.

Mee's early years were marked by a methodical approach to rebuilding the squad. He recognized that success would not come overnight and set about laying the groundwork for long-term achievement. His vision was clear: to restore Arsenal to the pinnacle of English football through hard work, strategic signings, and the development of young talent.

Building the Team: Key Signings and the Emergence of a New Generation

Mee's first task as Arsenal manager was to rebuild a team that had struggled for consistency throughout the 1960s. He began by identifying key areas that needed strengthening and sought out players who could bring both skill and stability to the squad. Mee's approach to building the team was a blend of astute signings and the nurturing of homegrown talent, which would ultimately form the backbone of Arsenal's success.

One of Mee's most significant signings was George Graham, who joined Arsenal from Chelsea in 1966.

Graham, a versatile midfielder known for his vision and technical ability, quickly became a central figure in Mee's plans. His experience and leadership on the field were invaluable as Mee looked to instill a winning mentality within the squad.

Another crucial addition was Bob McNab, a left-back who arrived from Huddersfield Town in 1966. McNab's defensive solidity and consistent performances made him a key part of Mee's strategy to build a strong, organized backline. Together with the emergence of Pat Rice, a product of Arsenal's youth system, McNab helped to form the defensive foundation that would be crucial to Arsenal's success in the coming years.

While experienced signings like Graham and McNab provided immediate impact, Mee also placed great importance on the development of young players. Arsenal's youth system began to produce a new generation of talent, with players like Ray Kennedy, Charlie George, and John Radford emerging as key figures in the first team. Mee gave these young players opportunities to prove themselves, and their contributions would soon prove vital.

By the end of the 1960s, Mee had assembled a team that was a mix of seasoned professionals and promising youngsters. This blend of experience and youthful energy was exactly what Arsenal needed to compete at the highest level. The team began to gel, showing signs of the potential that would soon be fully realized.

European Success: Winning the 1970 Fairs Cup

The first major breakthrough for Bertie Mee's Arsenal came in the 1969-70 season when the club embarked on a successful campaign in the Inter-Cities Fairs Cup, a precursor to the UEFA Cup. This competition provided Arsenal with the perfect platform to demonstrate the progress they had made under Mee's leadership.

Arsenal's run to the final was characterized by a series of hard-fought victories, including notable wins against Ajax and Dinamo Bacau. The team's performances in Europe reflected the discipline, resilience, and tactical acumen that Mee had instilled in his players. Arsenal reached the final, where they faced Anderlecht, one of the top teams in Belgium.

The first leg of the final, played in Brussels, saw Arsenal suffer a 3-1 defeat, leaving them with a daunting task in the return leg at Highbury. Despite the setback, Mee remained confident in his team's ability to overturn the deficit. His belief was rewarded in the second leg, as Arsenal produced a scintillating performance to win 3-0, securing a 4-3 aggregate victory and claiming their first European trophy.

The triumph in the Fairs Cup was a landmark moment for Arsenal. It was the club's first major trophy in 17 years and signaled that Arsenal were once again a force to be reckoned with. The victory also vindicated Bertie Mee's approach and provided the players with the confidence they needed to compete at the highest level.

The success in Europe laid the foundation for what would become one of the most memorable seasons in Arsenal's history. The Fairs Cup win demonstrated that the team was capable of achieving great things, and it set the stage for the historic double that would follow in the next season.

Chapter 16: The Double of 1971

The 1970-71 Campaign: A Detailed Look at Arsenal's Double-Winning Season

The 1970-71 season is one of the most celebrated in Arsenal's history, as the club achieved the rare and coveted double, winning both the First Division title and the FA Cup. This remarkable achievement was the culmination of years of hard work, planning, and development under Bertie Mee, and it marked Arsenal's return to the pinnacle of English football.

Arsenal's league campaign was characterized by consistency, resilience, and a strong defensive foundation. The team, built on the principles of discipline and teamwork that Mee had emphasized, proved to be incredibly difficult to break down. Arsenal conceded just 29 goals in 42 league matches, a testament to the solidity of their defense, which was anchored by captain Frank McLintock and goalkeeper Bob Wilson.

In attack, Arsenal were equally effective. The forward line, led by John Radford and Ray Kennedy, provided the goals that powered Arsenal's title challenge. Charlie George, a fan favorite and one of the brightest talents to emerge from Arsenal's youth system, added creativity and flair, while George Graham's experience and composure in midfield ensured that Arsenal remained competitive in every match.

The title race was a tight one, with Arsenal facing stiff competition from Leeds United, who were also vying for the top spot. The decisive moment came on the final day of the season, when Arsenal needed a result against Tottenham Hotspur at White Hart Lane to secure the league title. In a tense and closely contested match, Ray Kennedy scored the only goal, giving Arsenal a 1-0 victory and securing the First Division championship.

Just a few days later, Arsenal had the chance to complete the double in the FA Cup final against Liverpool. The match, played at Wembley Stadium, was another tense affair. After a goalless 90 minutes, the game went into extra time, where Liverpool took the lead. However, Arsenal's never-say-die attitude came to the fore, as Eddie Kelly equalized before Charlie George scored a stunning long-range goal to secure a 2-1 victory.

The double of 1971 was a monumental achievement for Arsenal and Bertie Mee. It was only the second time in the club's history that they had won the league, and the first time they had completed the double. The season marked the pinnacle of Mee's managerial career and solidified his place as one of the great figures in Arsenal's history.

Key Matches: Pivotal Games in the League and FA Cup

Several matches during the 1970-71 season were pivotal to Arsenal's success and are still remembered fondly by supporters.

1. **Arsenal 2-0 Manchester United (January 2, 1971):** This victory at Highbury was crucial in maintaining Arsenal's momentum in the title race. Goals from John Radford and George Graham secured a vital win against a strong Manchester United side, demonstrating Arsenal's credentials as serious contenders for the league title.

2. **Arsenal 2-1 Liverpool (March 27, 1971):** Another key victory came against Liverpool at Highbury. With both teams in the hunt for the title, Arsenal's win, courtesy of goals from Ray Kennedy and George Graham, was a significant step toward their ultimate triumph.

3. **Tottenham Hotspur 0-1 Arsenal (May 3, 1971):** The final league match of the season, where Arsenal needed a result to clinch the title. Ray Kennedy's late goal at White Hart Lane secured the victory and the championship, making this match one of the most iconic in Arsenal's history.

4. **FA Cup Final: Arsenal 2-1 Liverpool (May 8, 1971):** The FA Cup final was the crowning moment of the season. After going a goal down in extra time, Arsenal's resilience shone through with goals from Eddie Kelly and Charlie George, completing the double in dramatic fashion.

These matches were defining moments in Arsenal's journey to the double, each one contributing to the team's overall success and demonstrating the qualities that made them champions.

The Players Behind the Success: Profiles of Ray Kennedy, George Graham, and Others

The success of Arsenal's 1970-71 season was built on the contributions of a talented and cohesive squad. Several players played key roles in the team's achievements, each bringing unique qualities that complemented Bertie Mee's tactical approach.

Ray Kennedy was one of the standout performers of the season. A versatile forward, Kennedy's ability to play both as a striker and in midfield made him a crucial asset for the team. His goals, including the title-clinching strike against Tottenham, were vital to Arsenal's success. Kennedy's physical presence, combined with his intelligent movement and finishing ability, made him one of the most feared forwards in the league.

George Graham was another key figure in Arsenal's double-winning team. Known as "The Stroller" for his calm and composed style of play, Graham was the creative force in Arsenal's midfield. His vision and passing ability allowed him to dictate the tempo of matches, and his experience provided a steadying influence on the younger players in the squad. Graham's leadership on and off the pitch was instrumental in guiding Arsenal through the pressures of the title race.

Charlie George was the flair player in Arsenal's team, a local boy who had come through the club's youth system. George's creativity and ability to produce moments of brilliance made him a fan favorite. His winning goal in the FA Cup final, a stunning strike from outside the box, is one of the most iconic moments in Arsenal's history and epitomized his talent and confidence.

Frank McLintock was the captain and leader of the team. A tough and determined defender, McLintock's leadership qualities were unmatched. He marshaled the defense with authority and was a driving force behind Arsenal's success. McLintock's experience and determination were crucial in the title run-in, particularly in the final matches of the season.

Bob Wilson, Arsenal's goalkeeper, was another key figure in the double-winning team. Wilson's shot-stopping ability and command of his area provided the foundation for Arsenal's strong defensive record. His performances in both the league and FA Cup were consistently excellent, and he played a vital role in Arsenal's success.

Together, these players, along with the rest of the squad, formed a team that was greater than the sum of its parts. Under Bertie Mee's guidance, they achieved something extraordinary, securing a place in Arsenal's history as one of the club's greatest ever sides. The double of 1971 remains a defining moment in Arsenal's legacy, and the players who made it possible are still celebrated as legends at the club.

Chapter 17: Post-Double Decline (1972-1976)

The Struggles to Maintain Success: The Challenges Following the Double

After the euphoria of the 1970-71 double-winning season, Arsenal faced the difficult task of maintaining their success in the following years. The pressures of staying at the top in English football are immense, and the weight of expectation began to take its toll on the club. The immediate years after the double saw Arsenal struggle to replicate the consistency and dominance that had characterized their triumphs.

One of the key challenges Arsenal faced was the physical and mental toll on the players who had played pivotal roles in the double-winning campaign. The intensity of the 1970-71 season, coupled with the demands of competing on multiple fronts, led to fatigue and a spate of injuries among key players. The likes of Ray Kennedy, George Graham, and Charlie George, who had been instrumental in Arsenal's success, began to show signs of wear, and their form fluctuated as a result.

The departure of influential players also contributed to Arsenal's decline. In 1974, Ray Kennedy left the club to join Liverpool, where he would go on to enjoy further success. Kennedy's departure was a significant blow to Arsenal, as he had been one of the club's most reliable goal scorers and a vital part of the team's attacking threat. The loss of key players like Kennedy left a void that Arsenal struggled to fill.

Tactically, the team found it difficult to adapt as other clubs caught up with and countered the methods that had brought Arsenal success. The defensive solidity and disciplined approach that had been so effective began to falter as teams found ways to break down Arsenal's resistance. The club also struggled to refresh and rejuvenate the squad with new talent, leading to a gradual decline in performances.

As a result, Arsenal's league form suffered. The club finished 5th in the 1971-72 season, a respectable but disappointing follow-up to their title-winning campaign. Subsequent seasons saw further declines, with Arsenal slipping into mid-table obscurity. The inability to sustain the heights of 1971 was a source of frustration for both the club and its supporters, who had hoped that the double would mark the beginning of a new era of dominance.

Terry Neill Takes Over: The Appointment of Terry Neill and Early Years

By the mid-1970s, it was clear that Arsenal needed a new direction. In 1976, the club made the decision to appoint Terry Neill as manager, a former Arsenal player who had previously managed Hull City and Tottenham Hotspur. At just 34 years old, Neill was one of the youngest managers in English football, and his appointment was seen as a bold move by the Arsenal board.

Neill's appointment was met with a mix of optimism and skepticism. On one hand, his connection to the club and his youthful energy were seen as positives that could reinvigorate a team in need of fresh ideas. On the other hand, his relative inexperience as a manager raised concerns about whether he could handle the pressures of managing a club like Arsenal.

Neill's early years at Arsenal were marked by a focus on rebuilding the squad. He inherited a team that was in transition, with several key players from the double-winning side either having left or being past their peak. Neill recognized the need to bring in new talent and sought to blend experienced players with promising youngsters.

One of Neill's first significant signings was the acquisition of Malcolm Macdonald from Newcastle United in 1976. Macdonald, a prolific striker known as "Supermac," was brought in to provide the goals that Arsenal had been lacking. His arrival was a statement of intent from Neill, who aimed to restore Arsenal's attacking prowess.

Neill also placed a strong emphasis on youth development, giving opportunities to young players like Liam Brady, who would go on to become one of Arsenal's most influential figures. Brady, a supremely talented midfielder with exceptional vision and technical ability, was a key part of Neill's plans to rebuild Arsenal and challenge for honors.

Despite the challenges of taking over a club in decline, Neill's early years showed signs of promise. The team began to play with more energy and creativity, and there was a sense that Arsenal were slowly finding their way back to competitiveness. However, success would not come immediately, and the club had to endure several near misses before tasting glory again.

Cup Runs and Near Misses: Arsenal's Close Calls in Domestic Competitions

While Arsenal struggled to maintain consistency in the league during the mid-1970s, the club found some solace in cup competitions. The FA Cup, in particular, provided Arsenal with opportunities to compete for silverware, though these campaigns were often marked by frustration and heartbreak.

In the 1971-72 season, just a year after their double triumph, Arsenal reached the FA Cup final, where they faced Leeds United. The final, held at Wembley Stadium, was a tightly contested match that ended in disappointment for Arsenal. Leeds won 1-0, with Allan Clarke's header proving to be the difference. The defeat was a bitter pill to swallow for Arsenal, who had come so close to retaining the FA Cup and securing another major trophy.

Arsenal continued to enjoy cup runs in the following seasons but were unable to add to their trophy cabinet. In 1973, the club reached the semifinals of the FA Cup, only to be defeated by Sunderland, who would go on to win the competition. The pattern of near misses continued, with Arsenal frequently falling just short of success in domestic competitions.

These close calls were emblematic of Arsenal's struggles during the post-double decline. The team was capable of competing with the best on their day, but inconsistency and a lack of cutting edge in crucial moments often let them down. The frustration of coming so close to glory without securing it was palpable, both within the club and among the supporters.

However, these cup runs also provided valuable experience for the younger players in the squad, many of whom would play key roles in Arsenal's resurgence in the late 1970s. The lessons learned from these near misses would eventually contribute to the club's return to the top of English football.

Chapter 18: FA Cup Success and European Nights (1977-1979)

The 1978 FA Cup Final: Analysis of the Defeat to Ipswich Town

The 1977-78 season saw Arsenal reach the FA Cup final for the first time since their defeat to Leeds United in 1972. This time, the Gunners faced Ipswich Town, a team that was enjoying a period of success under the management of Bobby Robson. The final, held at Wembley Stadium, was eagerly anticipated by Arsenal fans who hoped that the club could end its trophy drought.

Despite being favorites going into the match, Arsenal struggled to impose themselves against a well-organized Ipswich side. Ipswich played with energy and confidence, disrupting Arsenal's rhythm and creating numerous chances. Arsenal, on the other hand, were uncharacteristically lethargic and failed to find their usual attacking fluency.

The decisive moment came in the 77th minute when Ipswich's Roger Osborne scored the only goal of the game, capitalizing on a defensive mistake by Arsenal. Ipswich's victory was well-deserved, as they had outplayed Arsenal for much of the match, hitting the woodwork three times before finally breaking the deadlock.

For Arsenal, the defeat was a major disappointment. The performance in the final was a stark contrast to the team's earlier displays in the competition, and the loss highlighted the inconsistency that had plagued the club in recent years. The defeat also raised questions about Arsenal's ability to perform in big matches, as the team once again fell short on the biggest stage.

However, the experience of reaching the final and the lessons learned from the defeat would prove valuable as Arsenal continued to rebuild under Terry Neill. The disappointment of the 1978 final set the stage for a renewed determination to succeed, and the club's response would be swift and decisive.

The 1979 FA Cup Win: A Thrilling Victory Against Manchester United

Arsenal's response to the disappointment of 1978 came in the form of a thrilling FA Cup campaign in the 1978-79 season. The team, galvanized by the previous year's defeat, embarked on a journey to Wembley with a renewed sense of purpose and determination.

The final, held on May 12, 1979, saw Arsenal face Manchester United, one of the most famous clubs in English football. The match is widely regarded as one of the greatest FA Cup finals of all time, due to the dramatic nature of the game and the quality of football on display.

Arsenal started the match brilliantly, racing to a 2-0 lead within the first 20 minutes thanks to goals from Brian Talbot and Frank Stapleton. The team played with confidence and composure, controlling the game and creating numerous chances to extend their lead. For much of the match, it appeared that Arsenal were on course for a comfortable victory.

However, the final took a dramatic turn in the closing minutes. Manchester United, refusing to give up, scored twice in quick succession through Gordon McQueen and Sammy McIlroy to level the score at 2-2. With just minutes remaining, it seemed as though Arsenal's hopes of lifting the FA Cup were slipping away.

But in one of the most memorable moments in FA Cup history, Arsenal responded immediately. With just seconds left on the clock, Alan Sunderland met a cross from Graham Rix at the far post to score the winning goal, securing a 3-2 victory for Arsenal. The dramatic finish sent the Arsenal supporters into raptures and secured the club's first major trophy since 1971.

The 1979 FA Cup win was a defining moment for Arsenal and for Terry Neill. It marked the culmination of the rebuilding process that had begun under Neill's leadership and was a testament to the team's resilience and determination. The victory also helped to restore Arsenal's status as one of the top clubs in English football, ending a decade-long wait for silverware.

European Adventures: Arsenal's Performances in European Competitions

While domestic success had eluded Arsenal for much of the 1970s, the club also made notable strides in European competition during this period. Arsenal's performances in the UEFA Cup and the European Cup Winners' Cup provided the team with valuable experience on the continental stage and added to the club's growing reputation.

In the 1978-79 season, Arsenal competed in the UEFA Cup, where they reached the quarterfinals before being eliminated by Red Star Belgrade. The team's performances in Europe were marked by a mix of solid defensive displays and moments of attacking brilliance, but they ultimately fell short against a strong Red Star side. Despite the disappointment, the experience of playing against top European opposition helped to further develop the squad.

The following season, Arsenal competed in the European Cup Winners' Cup, a competition they had won in 1970. The team enjoyed a strong run, reaching the semifinals before being knocked out by Juventus. The tie against Juventus was a closely contested affair, with Arsenal losing 2-1 on aggregate. The narrow defeat was a reminder of the fine margins that often separate success and failure in European football.

Although Arsenal did not add to their trophy cabinet in Europe during this period, their performances were encouraging and demonstrated the club's ability to compete on multiple fronts. The experience gained in European competitions helped to strengthen the squad and provided the players with the belief that they could succeed at the highest level.

The late 1970s were a period of transition and rebuilding for Arsenal, but the success in the FA Cup and the experiences in Europe laid the foundation for future achievements. The club had emerged from a difficult period with renewed confidence and a sense of purpose, and the stage was set for further successes in the years to come.

Chapter 19: The Early Graham Years (1986-1989)

George Graham's Philosophy: Defensive Solidity and Tactical Discipline

When George Graham was appointed as Arsenal's manager in May 1986, the club was in desperate need of direction and a return to its winning ways. The team had struggled with inconsistency and had been without a major trophy since the 1979 FA Cup victory. Graham, a former Arsenal player who had been part of the club's successful sides in the late 1960s and early 1970s, was seen as the man to restore discipline and instill a winning mentality.

From the outset, Graham's philosophy was clear: his Arsenal team would be built on a foundation of defensive solidity and tactical discipline. He believed that a strong defense was the cornerstone of any successful side, and he was determined to mold Arsenal into a team that was difficult to break down. This focus on defense was not just about keeping clean sheets; it was about controlling games, frustrating opponents, and creating a platform from which the team could launch effective attacks.

Graham's approach was rooted in a meticulous attention to detail. He was a hands-on manager who took charge of training sessions, drilling his players in their defensive responsibilities and ensuring that they understood their roles within the team. Every player was expected to work hard, track back, and contribute to the team's defensive shape. This collective commitment to defense became a hallmark of Graham's Arsenal, and it was a philosophy that would define his tenure.

Offensively, Graham favored a pragmatic style of play that prioritized efficiency over flair. He valued players who could execute his game plan with precision, and he was willing to sacrifice individual creativity for the sake of the team's overall structure. This approach earned him the nickname "Stroller" during his playing days, and as a manager, he carried the same cool, calculated demeanor. Graham's Arsenal was a team that knew how to grind out results, and while they might not always have played the most attractive football, they were effective and, ultimately, successful.

First Successes: The 1987 League Cup Victory

Graham's methods quickly began to bear fruit, and in just his first full season as manager, he guided Arsenal to their first major trophy in eight years. The 1986-87 League Cup campaign was a turning point for the club, as it provided the team with a taste of success and laid the foundation for future triumphs.

Arsenal's journey to the League Cup final was marked by a series of hard-fought victories, including a memorable semifinal win over Tottenham Hotspur. The semifinal was a two-legged affair, with Arsenal winning 2-1 at Highbury before securing a 2-1 victory at White Hart Lane, with goals from Viv Anderson and Niall Quinn sending Arsenal through to the final. The victory over their fierce North London rivals was particularly sweet and gave the team a huge boost of confidence heading into the final.

The League Cup final, played at Wembley Stadium on April 5, 1987, saw Arsenal face Liverpool, one of the dominant forces in English football at the time. Liverpool were the favorites, having enjoyed considerable success both domestically and in Europe throughout the 1980s. However, Graham's Arsenal were undaunted, and they approached the match with the same discipline and determination that had characterized their season.

The final began poorly for Arsenal, as Liverpool took the lead through a goal from Ian Rush in the 23rd minute. At that point, Liverpool's record when Rush scored was formidable—they had never lost a match in which he had found the net. But Arsenal, showing the resilience that would become a trademark of Graham's teams, fought back. Charlie Nicholas, a player known for his flair and finishing ability, equalized for Arsenal in the 40th minute, setting up a tense second half.

With the match finely poised, Nicholas struck again in the 83rd minute, his deflected shot finding the back of the net to give Arsenal a 2-1 lead. The Gunners held on to claim the victory, securing their first League Cup title. The triumph was a significant moment for the club and for Graham, who had delivered silverware in his first season in charge. It also demonstrated that Arsenal were capable of competing with the best, even when they were not the favorites.

The 1987 League Cup victory was more than just a trophy; it was a statement of intent. It showed that Arsenal were back as a force in English football and that Graham's methods were beginning to yield results. The win instilled a winning mentality within the squad and set the stage for further successes in the years to come.

Building a Defensive Fortress: The Formation of the Famous Back Four

One of George Graham's most enduring legacies at Arsenal was the formation of the club's famous back four, a defensive unit that would become synonymous with the club's success throughout the late 1980s and early 1990s. Graham's commitment to defensive excellence led him to assemble a group of players who would become the bedrock of his team.

The back four consisted of Tony Adams, Lee Dixon, Steve Bould, and Nigel Winterburn, with David O'Leary and Martin Keown also playing crucial roles during this period. Each player brought something unique to the defensive line, and together, they formed one of the most formidable defenses in English football history.

Tony Adams, who had made his debut for Arsenal in 1983, was the natural leader of the back four. Tall, strong, and commanding, Adams was the epitome of a traditional English center-half. His ability to read the game, organize the defense, and inspire his teammates made him an indispensable figure in Graham's side. Adams was appointed club captain at the age of 21, a testament to his leadership qualities and the trust Graham placed in him.

Lee Dixon and **Nigel Winterburn** were the full-backs, providing both defensive stability and the ability to support the attack when needed. Dixon, who joined Arsenal from Stoke City in 1988, was a right-back known for his consistency and reliability. Winterburn, who had been signed from Wimbledon in 1987, was equally adept on the left side, combining tenacity with a good positional sense. Both players were vital to Graham's tactical setup, as they were capable of defending in wide areas while also contributing to Arsenal's counter-attacking play.

Steve Bould, who arrived from Stoke City in 1988, was the perfect partner for Adams in central defense. Bould's height, strength, and aerial ability complemented Adams' leadership and positional awareness. Together, they formed a formidable central defensive partnership that was difficult for opponents to break down.

David O'Leary and **Martin Keown** also played crucial roles during this period. O'Leary, who had been with Arsenal since the 1970s, brought experience and composure to the defense, while Keown, who rejoined Arsenal in 1993 after an earlier spell at the club, added grit and determination.

Graham's meticulous coaching ensured that the back four operated as a cohesive unit. He drilled them relentlessly in training, focusing on their positioning, communication, and understanding of the offside trap. The result was a defense that was almost telepathic in its understanding, with each player knowing exactly where to be and what to do at any given moment.

The famous back four became the cornerstone of Arsenal's success under Graham. Their ability to keep clean sheets and frustrate opponents allowed the team to win matches by narrow margins, often by a single goal. The defensive solidity they provided gave Arsenal the platform to compete for and win trophies, and their legacy remains one of the most celebrated aspects of Arsenal's history.

Chapter 20: The 1989 Title Triumph

The 1988-89 League Campaign: Arsenal's Pursuit of the Title

The 1988-89 season is one of the most storied in Arsenal's history, culminating in one of the most dramatic title races English football has ever seen. Arsenal entered the season with confidence, buoyed by their recent successes under George Graham. The team was well-drilled, defensively solid, and had begun to develop an attacking edge that made them genuine title contenders.

From the outset, Arsenal demonstrated their intent to challenge for the First Division title. The team was consistent throughout the season, with standout performances from key players such as Alan Smith, who would go on to win the Golden Boot as the league's top scorer, and Paul Merson, whose creativity and flair added a new dimension to Arsenal's attack.

Arsenal's defensive strength, anchored by the famous back four of Dixon, Adams, Bould, and Winterburn, was crucial to their campaign. The team kept 15 clean sheets over the course of the season, frustrating opponents with their disciplined and organized play. Arsenal's ability to grind out results, even in tough matches, kept them in the title race throughout the season.

As the season progressed, it became clear that the title would be contested between Arsenal and Liverpool, the reigning champions and the dominant force in English football during the 1980s. Liverpool had a star-studded squad, and their experience in title races made them formidable opponents. However, Arsenal matched them step for step, and the two teams began to pull away from the rest of the pack.

The title race came to a head in the final weeks of the season. Arsenal, who had led the table for much of the campaign, suffered a dip in form that allowed Liverpool to overtake them. By the time the final match of the season arrived, Arsenal found themselves three points behind Liverpool, who also had a superior goal difference. To win the title, Arsenal needed to beat Liverpool by at least two goals in the final match at Anfield—a daunting task, given Liverpool's formidable home record.

The Final Day at Anfield: A Blow-by-Blow Account of the Historic Victory

The final match of the 1988-89 season, played on May 26, 1989, at Anfield, is etched into football folklore. Arsenal's task was clear: they needed to win by two clear goals to claim the First Division title. Anything less would see Liverpool crowned champions once again.

The atmosphere at Anfield was electric, with Liverpool's supporters confident that their team would secure the title. Arsenal's players, however, were determined to defy the odds. George Graham had drilled his team meticulously in the lead-up to the match, and they approached the game with a steely resolve.

The first half was tense and cagey, with neither side able to break the deadlock. Arsenal, knowing they needed to score twice, were disciplined in their approach, ensuring they did not concede an early goal that would have made their task even more difficult. As the halftime whistle blew, the score remained 0-0, and Arsenal's hopes hung in the balance.

Early in the second half, Arsenal found the breakthrough they desperately needed. In the 52nd minute, a free-kick from the right was swung into the box, and Alan Smith rose to meet it with a glancing header that found the back of the net. The goal stunned the Anfield crowd and gave Arsenal belief that they could achieve the improbable. However, they still needed one more goal to claim the title.

As the minutes ticked away, the tension on the pitch and in the stands grew palpable. Arsenal pressed forward, but Liverpool's defense held firm, knowing that a single goal conceded would cost them the title. With just moments remaining, it seemed that Arsenal's efforts would fall agonizingly short.

Then, in the dying seconds of the match, Arsenal produced one of the most iconic moments in football history. Michael Thomas, a dynamic midfielder known for his energy and drive, made a surging run from midfield. After a quick one-two with Alan Smith, the ball broke kindly for Thomas, who found himself bearing down on goal. As Liverpool goalkeeper Bruce Grobbelaar rushed out to meet him, Thomas kept his composure and coolly lifted the ball over the onrushing keeper and into the net.

The goal, scored in the 91st minute, secured a 2-0 victory for Arsenal and the First Division title. The scenes that followed were unforgettable. Arsenal's players and fans erupted in celebration, while Liverpool's supporters were left in stunned silence. The title had been won in the most dramatic fashion possible, and Michael Thomas's goal became the defining moment of Arsenal's season.

Aftermath and Legacy: The Long-Term Impact of the 1989 Title Win

The 1989 title triumph was a watershed moment for Arsenal. It marked the club's first league title since 1971 and was achieved in a manner that ensured it would be remembered as one of the greatest moments in English football history. The victory at Anfield not only secured the championship but also signaled a new era for Arsenal under George Graham.

The triumph solidified Graham's reputation as one of the top managers in the country. His emphasis on discipline, defensive organization, and tactical acumen had paid off, and he had guided Arsenal to the pinnacle of English football. The success also validated his approach to the game, which prioritized results over style—a philosophy that would define Arsenal's play throughout his tenure.

The 1989 title win also had a lasting impact on the players who were part of that team. Tony Adams, who captained the side, became an Arsenal legend, leading the club to further successes in the years that followed. Michael Thomas's dramatic goal secured his place in Arsenal folklore, and the members of the famous back four—Dixon, Bould, Adams, and Winterburn—became the bedrock of one of the most formidable defenses in English football.

For Arsenal supporters, the 1989 title win was a source of immense pride and joy. It was a moment that encapsulated the highs and lows of football, and it created memories that would be cherished for generations. The victory at Anfield became a symbol of Arsenal's resilience and determination, qualities that would continue to define the club in the years to come.

The legacy of the 1989 title win extended beyond the immediate celebrations. It set the stage for Arsenal's continued success under George Graham, with the club going on to win more domestic and European honors in the early 1990s. The triumph also reinforced Arsenal's status as one of the leading clubs in English football, a position they would maintain and build upon in the years that followed.

In the broader context of English football, the 1989 title race is remembered as one of the most exciting and dramatic in history. It showcased the unpredictability and excitement of the game, and it remains a touchstone for fans and players alike. For Arsenal, it was the beginning of a new chapter of success, one that would see the club continue to compete at the highest levels both domestically and in Europe.

Chapter 21: Continued Success and Controversies (1990-1993)

The 1990-91 Title: Winning the League with Only One Defeat

The 1990-91 season stands as one of Arsenal's finest in the history of English football. Under the management of George Graham, the team embarked on a campaign that saw them dominate the First Division, winning the league title in emphatic fashion while losing just one match all season. This achievement highlighted the strength and resilience of Graham's Arsenal, a team that was built on the principles of discipline, organization, and defensive solidity.

Arsenal began the season with a sense of purpose, having narrowly missed out on the title in the previous campaign. From the outset, it was clear that Graham's side was determined to reclaim their place at the top of English football. The team's defensive unit, led by captain Tony Adams, was imperious, conceding only 18 goals in 38 matches—a record that underscored the tactical acumen of Graham's management.

Key to Arsenal's success was the formidable back four, which by now had become legendary. The defensive line of Lee Dixon, Steve Bould, Tony

Adams, and Nigel Winterburn, with David Seaman as the goalkeeper, was virtually impenetrable. This defensive solidity allowed Arsenal to grind out results, even in matches where their attacking play was less fluent.

Offensively, Arsenal were led by the striking partnership of Alan Smith and Paul Merson, who provided the goals needed to secure crucial victories. Smith, in particular, was in prolific form, finishing as the league's top scorer and playing a pivotal role in many of Arsenal's wins.

One of the most significant matches of the season was the 1-0 victory over Liverpool at Anfield, a ground where Arsenal had famously won the title in 1989. The win was a testament to the team's ability to perform under pressure and against top opposition. Another crucial moment came in February 1991, when Arsenal suffered their only league defeat of the season, a 2-1 loss to Chelsea at Stamford Bridge. Despite this setback, the team quickly regrouped and went unbeaten for the remainder of the season.

Arsenal clinched the title with two games to spare, finishing with 83 points, seven points clear of second-placed Liverpool. The triumph was a testament to the effectiveness of Graham's methods and the quality of the squad he had assembled.

Winning the league with just one defeat was a remarkable achievement and further cemented Arsenal's reputation as one of the best teams in the country.

Domestic and European Cups: The 1993 FA Cup and League Cup Double

Following their league triumph in 1991, Arsenal continued to enjoy success in domestic cup competitions. The 1992-93 season was particularly notable as Arsenal became the first English club to win both the FA Cup and the League Cup in the same season, completing a historic domestic cup double.

The League Cup, known at the time as the Coca-Cola Cup, saw Arsenal embark on a campaign that culminated in a final against Sheffield Wednesday at Wembley Stadium. The final, played on April 18, 1993, was a tightly contested affair. Arsenal took the lead through a goal from Paul Merson, but Sheffield Wednesday equalized, forcing the match into extra time. With the game seemingly heading for a replay, Arsenal's Steve Morrow scored the winning goal, securing a 2-1 victory and the club's second League Cup trophy under George Graham.

Just over a month later, Arsenal faced Sheffield Wednesday again, this time in the FA Cup final. The final, held on May 15, 1993, was another closely fought match. The game ended 1-1, with Ian Wright scoring for Arsenal and David Hirst equalizing for Sheffield Wednesday, leading to a replay—the last FA Cup final replay in history—held five days later. In the replay, Wright once again put Arsenal ahead, but Wednesday equalized through Chris Waddle. The match appeared to be heading for extra time when, in the final moments, Andy Linighan scored a dramatic header to give Arsenal a 2-1 victory and their first FA Cup under Graham.

The double cup triumph was a significant achievement for Arsenal and George Graham. It demonstrated the team's ability to succeed in knockout competitions and reinforced Graham's reputation as a manager who could deliver trophies. The victories were also a testament to the squad's depth and resilience, as Arsenal had to navigate a demanding fixture schedule and overcome strong opposition to secure both titles.

The Scandal and Graham's Departure: The Bung Scandal That Ended Graham's Reign

Despite the success on the pitch, George Graham's tenure at Arsenal came to an abrupt and controversial end in 1995. The scandal that led to his departure centered around illegal payments, known as "bungs," which Graham had received in connection with player transfers.

The scandal came to light in February 1995 when it was revealed that Graham had accepted £425,000 from Norwegian agent Rune Hauge in relation to the transfers of Danish players John Jensen and Pål Lydersen to Arsenal. The payments were made without the knowledge of the club, and when the details emerged, it caused a significant uproar within the football community.

The revelations led to an investigation by the Football Association, which ultimately found Graham guilty of misconduct. In February 1995, Arsenal made the difficult decision to part ways with Graham, terminating his contract with immediate effect. The scandal tarnished Graham's legacy at Arsenal and marked a sad end to what had been a highly successful managerial career at the club.

Graham's departure was a major blow to Arsenal, as he had been the architect of much of the club's success during the late 1980s and early 1990s. Under his guidance, Arsenal had won two league titles, an FA Cup, two League Cups, and a European trophy. However, the scandal overshadowed these achievements and left the club in a state of uncertainty.

The bung scandal also had wider implications for English football, leading to increased scrutiny of transfer dealings and the conduct of managers and agents. It highlighted the need for greater transparency and regulation within the game and prompted reforms aimed at preventing similar incidents in the future.

For Arsenal, the immediate challenge was to move forward and find a new manager who could restore stability to the club and build on the foundation that Graham had established. The post-Graham era would be a period of transition, as the club sought to navigate the challenges of a changing football landscape.

Chapter 22: The Post-Graham Transition (1994-1996)

Cup Winners' Cup Glory: The 1994 European Triumph

Before the scandal that led to George Graham's departure, Arsenal enjoyed one of their most memorable European successes under his management. The 1993-94 season saw Arsenal win the European Cup Winners' Cup, their second major European trophy, following their triumph in the 1970 Fairs Cup.

Arsenal's Cup Winners' Cup campaign began with victories over Odense BK, Standard Liège, and Torino, setting up a semifinal clash with French club Paris Saint-Germain. After a hard-fought 1-1 draw in Paris, Arsenal secured their place in the final with a 1-0 victory at Highbury, thanks to a goal from Kevin Campbell.

The final, played in Copenhagen on May 4, 1994, saw Arsenal face Italian giants Parma, a team that boasted some of the best players in Europe, including Gianfranco Zola, Faustino Asprilla, and Tomas Brolin. Despite being underdogs, Arsenal produced a disciplined and determined performance, epitomizing the defensive solidity that had become their hallmark under Graham.

Arsenal took the lead in the 21st minute through a goal from Alan Smith, who struck a superb left-footed volley from outside the box. The goal was enough to secure a 1-0 victory, as Arsenal's defense, led by Tony Adams, Steve Bould, and David Seaman, withstood relentless pressure from Parma's attack.

The victory was a significant achievement for Arsenal, marking their first European trophy in over two decades. It also demonstrated the strength of Graham's tactical approach, which prioritized defensive organization and the ability to capitalize on opportunities. The triumph in Copenhagen was one of the highlights of Graham's tenure and provided a fitting end to his time at Arsenal.

The Interregnum: The Club's Direction Under Temporary Managers

In the wake of George Graham's departure, Arsenal found themselves in a period of transition, with the club's direction uncertain. Stewart Houston, Graham's assistant manager, was appointed as caretaker manager for the remainder of the 1994-95 season. Houston, who had worked closely with Graham, sought to maintain continuity and stability within the squad, but the team's performances were inconsistent.

Despite the challenges, Houston guided Arsenal to the final of the 1995 Cup Winners' Cup, where they faced Spanish side Real Zaragoza. The final, played in Paris, was a tightly contested match that ended in heartbreak for Arsenal. With the score tied at 1-1 after 90 minutes, the game went into extra time. In the dying moments, Zaragoza's Nayim scored a dramatic goal from near the halfway line, lobbing David Seaman to secure a 2-1 victory for the Spanish side.

The defeat was a bitter pill to swallow for Arsenal, as it denied them the chance to defend their European title. However, Houston's ability to lead the team to another European final was commendable, given the turmoil that had followed Graham's departure.

In the summer of 1995, Arsenal appointed Bruce Rioch as the new permanent manager. Rioch, who had previously managed Middlesbrough and Bolton Wanderers, was tasked with restoring stability and guiding Arsenal back to the top of English football. One of Rioch's most significant contributions was the signing of Dutch forward Dennis Bergkamp from Inter Milan. Bergkamp's arrival signaled a shift in Arsenal's approach, as the club sought to add more flair and creativity to their attack.

However, Rioch's tenure at Arsenal was short-lived. Despite guiding the team to a fifth-place finish in the

1995-96 Premier League season, tensions between Rioch and the Arsenal board, particularly over transfer policy and player recruitment, led to his departure after just one season in charge.

The interregnum period was marked by uncertainty and a lack of direction, as Arsenal struggled to find the right managerial leadership. The club's fortunes on the pitch were mixed, and there was a sense that Arsenal needed a fresh start to regain their place among the elite of English football.

Preparing for Wenger: The Conditions Leading to Arsène Wenger's Appointment

As Arsenal entered the 1996-97 season, the club was at a crossroads. The departure of Bruce Rioch left the managerial position vacant once again, and the Arsenal board was determined to find a long-term solution that would provide stability and success. It was against this backdrop that the club began to look beyond the traditional pool of British managers and consider a more radical appointment.

The conditions leading to Arsène Wenger's appointment were shaped by several factors. First, there was a growing recognition within the club that the football landscape was changing, with European influences becoming more prominent. The success of foreign managers and players in the Premier

League had demonstrated the value of a more diverse approach, and Arsenal was keen to embrace this trend.

Second, the club's recent history had been marked by defensive solidity and tactical discipline, but there was a desire to add more creativity and attacking flair to the team's style of play. The signing of Dennis Bergkamp had been a step in this direction, and the Arsenal board was looking for a manager who could build on this foundation and take the club to the next level.

Third, Arsenal's financial situation had improved, thanks in part to the success of the Premier League and the club's prudent management. This financial stability allowed Arsenal to consider a long-term project that would involve significant investment in both the squad and the club's infrastructure.

It was in this context that Arsenal identified Arsène Wenger, then managing in Japan with Nagoya Grampus Eight, as the man to lead the club into a new era. Wenger's reputation as a forward-thinking coach, with a deep understanding of the game and a commitment to developing young talent, made him an attractive candidate. His success in France with AS Monaco, where he had won the league title and nurtured players like George Weah and Youri Djorkaeff, further bolstered his credentials.

Wenger's appointment in October 1996 was met with curiosity and skepticism in equal measure. He was relatively unknown in England, and his methods were unconventional by the standards of English football at the time. However, the Arsenal board, led by chairman David Dein, was convinced that Wenger was the right man to take the club forward.

The conditions were now set for a new chapter in Arsenal's history, one that would be defined by innovation, success, and a transformation in the club's identity. Arsène Wenger's arrival would mark the beginning of one of the most successful and influential periods in the history of Arsenal Football Club.

Chapter 23: Return to Silverware (2014-2017)

Ending the Drought: The 2014 FA Cup Victory and Its Importance

By the time Arsenal reached the 2014 FA Cup final, the club had endured a nine-year trophy drought that weighed heavily on the players, the management, and the fans. Arsène Wenger, who had led Arsenal to numerous titles in his early years, was under immense pressure to deliver silverware and silence critics who questioned whether he could still lead the club to success.

The 2013-2014 season had seen Arsenal show promise, with the team leading the Premier League table for much of the season before fading in the title race. However, their performance in the FA Cup provided a crucial opportunity to end the long wait for a trophy. Arsenal's journey to the final included hard-fought victories against Liverpool and Everton, setting up a final clash with Hull City at Wembley Stadium on May 17, 2014.

The final began disastrously for Arsenal. Hull City, seen by many as underdogs, shocked the Gunners by scoring twice within the first eight minutes, leaving Arsenal 2-0 down and facing the very real prospect of another trophy-less season. The atmosphere among the Arsenal faithful was tense, but the players, led by captain Mikel Arteta, showed resilience and determination to fight back.

Arsenal began to regain control of the match, and in the 17th minute, Santi Cazorla provided a moment of magic, curling a free-kick into the top corner to reduce the deficit to 2-1. The goal lifted the team and the fans, and Arsenal pressed forward in search of an equalizer. It eventually came in the 71st minute when Laurent Koscielny scrambled the ball home following a corner, bringing Arsenal level at 2-2.

The match went into extra time, with both teams battling fatigue and nerves. In the 109th minute, Aaron Ramsey scored the decisive goal, finishing a move with a first-time strike that sent the Arsenal fans into ecstasy. The final whistle confirmed a 3-2 victory for Arsenal, ending the long trophy drought and giving Wenger his fifth FA Cup title.

The 2014 FA Cup victory was more than just a trophy; it was a symbolic moment that marked the end of years of frustration and near-misses. For Wenger, it was a vindication of his philosophy and methods, which had been questioned during the barren years. The win also provided the players with the belief that they could compete for and win major honors, setting the stage for further successes in the coming years.

FA Cup Dominance: Winning Three FA Cups in Four Years (2014, 2015, 2017)

Following the 2014 FA Cup triumph, Arsenal entered a period of domestic cup dominance, winning two more FA Cups in the next three years. This remarkable run of success in the competition underscored Wenger's ability to navigate the challenges of knockout football and solidified his legacy as one of the greatest managers in the history of the FA Cup.

The 2014-2015 season saw Arsenal build on their previous success by reaching the FA Cup final once again. This time, they faced Aston Villa in the final, held at Wembley on May 30, 2015. Arsenal were overwhelming favorites, and they delivered a commanding performance. Theo Walcott opened the scoring with a well-taken goal, and Alexis Sánchez doubled the lead with a stunning long-range strike. Further goals from Per Mertesacker and Olivier Giroud sealed a 4-0 victory, giving Arsenal their 12th FA Cup and making Wenger the most successful manager in the competition's history at that time, with six FA Cup wins.

The 2016-2017 season brought another FA Cup run, culminating in a final against Chelsea, who had just won the Premier League title and were aiming to complete the double. The final, played on May 27,

2017, was one of Arsenal's most memorable performances under Wenger. Despite being underdogs, Arsenal started the match brilliantly, with Alexis Sánchez scoring in the fourth minute. Chelsea equalized through Diego Costa, but Aaron Ramsey, as he had done in 2014, scored the winning goal just moments later, heading home from an Olivier Giroud cross to secure a 2-1 victory.

The victory over Chelsea not only gave Arsenal their 13th FA Cup—making them the most successful club in the competition's history—but also highlighted Wenger's enduring ability to inspire his teams in the biggest moments. Winning three FA Cups in four years was a remarkable achievement, especially given the intense competition in English football during this period.

These cup victories provided Arsenal with much-needed silverware during a time when Premier League and European success proved elusive. They also served as a reminder of Wenger's expertise in cup competitions and his knack for delivering trophies even in the face of adversity. The FA Cups were cherished by the fans, who reveled in the club's continued ability to win on the grand stage of Wembley.

Wenger's Legacy: Evaluating Wenger's Long-Term Impact on Arsenal and English Football

Arsène Wenger's tenure as Arsenal manager spanned over two decades, during which he transformed the club and left an indelible mark on English football. While the latter years of his reign were marked by intense scrutiny and debate, particularly regarding the club's performance in the Premier League and Europe, Wenger's legacy is one of profound influence and lasting impact.

Wenger arrived at Arsenal in 1996 as a relatively unknown figure in English football, but he quickly established himself as a visionary manager. His approach to the game, characterized by a commitment to attacking football, technical excellence, and innovative training methods, revolutionized not only Arsenal but also the Premier League. Wenger's emphasis on nutrition, fitness, and the professional development of players set new standards that were soon adopted by clubs across the country.

One of Wenger's most significant contributions was his ability to develop and nurture young talent. During his tenure, he oversaw the emergence of several generations of players who became key figures at Arsenal and in world football. Players like Thierry Henry, Patrick Vieira, Cesc Fàbregas, and

Robin van Persie all flourished under Wenger's guidance, and his eye for talent helped Arsenal remain competitive even during periods of financial constraint.

Wenger's influence extended beyond the pitch. His commitment to playing attractive, possession-based football helped to change the perception of the English game, which had traditionally been associated with physicality and direct play. Wenger's Arsenal teams, particularly the "Invincibles" of the 2003-2004 season, were celebrated for their style, fluidity, and technical prowess, earning admiration from fans and pundits alike.

The latter years of Wenger's reign were more challenging, as the club struggled to compete financially with the likes of Chelsea, Manchester City, and Manchester United. Despite these challenges, Wenger managed to keep Arsenal in the upper echelons of English football, securing regular top-four finishes and leading the club to several FA Cup victories. His ability to consistently qualify for the Champions League, even without the financial resources of his rivals, was a testament to his managerial acumen.

Wenger's legacy at Arsenal is also intertwined with the club's move to the Emirates Stadium, a project that he supported and helped to manage. The move from Highbury to the Emirates was a significant undertaking, and while it placed financial constraints on the club in the short term, it ensured Arsenal's long-term viability as a major footballing institution.

Critics of Wenger often pointed to the lack of Premier League titles in his later years and the club's struggles in Europe, but his overall contribution to Arsenal and English football cannot be understated. Wenger's philosophy of developing young players, his commitment to attractive football, and his influence on the modernization of the Premier League have left a lasting legacy that continues to shape the game.

As Wenger stepped down as Arsenal manager in 2018, he left behind a club that had been transformed under his leadership. His impact on Arsenal was profound, and his influence on English football will be remembered for generations to come. While the latter years of his tenure were marked by challenges and debates, Wenger's legacy is one of innovation, success, and a deep commitment to the values of the game. He remains one of the most respected and admired figures in football, both in England and around the world.

Chapter 24: The Final Years of Wenger (2017-2018)

Challenges in the League: Struggles to Compete with Emerging Giants like Manchester City and Chelsea

As the 2017-2018 season approached, Arsène Wenger found himself facing perhaps the most challenging period of his managerial career. The landscape of the Premier League had changed dramatically since Wenger's early years at Arsenal. Clubs like Manchester City and Chelsea, backed by immense financial resources, had emerged as dominant forces, making it increasingly difficult for Arsenal to compete for the Premier League title.

The 2016-2017 season had ended on a disappointing note for Arsenal, as they finished outside the top four for the first time under Wenger's leadership, missing out on Champions League qualification. The pressure was mounting on Wenger to deliver results in the league, but the 2017-2018 campaign brought further struggles. Arsenal's inconsistent performances and defensive frailties saw them fall behind the leading pack, and the gap between Arsenal and the Premier League's top teams widened.

Manchester City, under the guidance of Pep Guardiola, were setting new standards in the league, playing an expansive, high-tempo style of football that left many of their rivals—including Arsenal—trailing in their wake. Chelsea, led by Antonio Conte, had also become a formidable force, while Manchester United and Liverpool were resurgent under José Mourinho and Jürgen Klopp, respectively.

Arsenal's struggles in the league were characterized by a lack of consistency and an inability to compete against the top sides. The Gunners often faltered in key matches against their rivals, with defensive lapses and a lack of cohesion in midfield contributing to their difficulties. Despite having talented players like Mesut Özil, Alexis Sánchez, and Alexandre Lacazette, Arsenal struggled to find the balance needed to challenge for the title.

The club's decline in the league standings was a source of frustration for the fans, many of whom had grown accustomed to competing for the Premier League crown in Wenger's early years. The sense of disillusionment among the supporters grew as Arsenal's hopes of reclaiming their place at the top of English football seemed increasingly distant.

European Campaigns: The 2017 Europa League Final and Other European Runs

While Arsenal's domestic league form was disappointing, their performances in European competitions offered some solace. After finishing fifth in the Premier League in the 2016-2017 season, Arsenal found themselves competing in the UEFA Europa League rather than the Champions League for the first time in two decades.

The 2017-2018 Europa League campaign was seen as an opportunity for Arsenal to secure silverware and qualify for the Champions League through the back door. Wenger prioritized the competition, fielding strong lineups throughout the tournament as Arsenal navigated their way through the group stage and knockout rounds.

Arsenal's European campaign included impressive victories over AC Milan in the round of 16 and CSKA Moscow in the quarterfinals, setting up a semifinal clash with Spanish giants Atlético Madrid. The first leg, played at the Emirates Stadium, saw Arsenal dominate much of the match but fail to capitalize on their chances, ultimately drawing 1-1 after a late equalizer from Atlético's Antoine Griezmann.

The second leg in Madrid was a tense affair. Arsenal needed a victory to reach the final, but they were unable to break down Atlético's resolute defense. A goal from Diego Costa gave Atlético a 1-0 win on the night and a 2-1 aggregate victory, ending Arsenal's hopes of European glory.

The disappointment of the Europa League exit was compounded by the knowledge that Arsenal's absence from the Champions League would extend for another season. Wenger, who had consistently led Arsenal into Europe's premier competition for nearly two decades, now faced the reality of Arsenal's diminished status on the European stage.

Wenger's Farewell: The Decision to Step Down and the Emotional End of an Era

As the 2017-2018 season drew to a close, speculation about Arsène Wenger's future reached a fever pitch. The growing dissatisfaction among fans, combined with the team's struggles in the league and Europe, created an atmosphere of uncertainty around the club. On April 20, 2018, Wenger announced that he would step down as Arsenal manager at the end of the season, bringing an end to his 22-year tenure at the club.

The decision marked the end of an era not only for Arsenal but for English football as a whole. Wenger's influence on the game had been profound, and his departure was met with a mix of emotions from fans, players, and pundits alike. For many, Wenger's decision to step down was seen as a necessary step to allow the club to move forward and rebuild under new leadership. However, it was also a deeply emotional moment, as Wenger had become synonymous with Arsenal and had shaped the club's identity over two decades.

Wenger's final home game in charge of Arsenal, a 5-0 victory over Burnley on May 6, 2018, was a poignant occasion. The match was followed by a heartfelt tribute to Wenger, with the players, staff, and supporters expressing their gratitude for his contributions to the club. Wenger, visibly moved by the reception, addressed the crowd, thanking them for their support and expressing his love for the club.

Wenger's farewell was a moment of reflection for Arsenal fans, many of whom had grown up watching his teams play and had experienced the highs and lows of his tenure. While the final years had been challenging, there was an overwhelming sense of appreciation for the legacy Wenger had built at Arsenal.

Legacy Debate: The Mixed Feelings Among Fans About Wenger's Legacy

As the dust settled on Wenger's departure, the debate over his legacy began in earnest. For some, Wenger's achievements were unparalleled, and he was rightly regarded as one of the greatest managers in the history of English football. His influence on the modern game, his commitment to attractive football, and his role in developing young talent were all seen as defining aspects of his legacy.

Wenger's early years at Arsenal, particularly the period between 1996 and 2004, were marked by unprecedented success. The "Invincibles" season, the double-winning campaigns, and the move to the Emirates Stadium were all high points that solidified Wenger's place in Arsenal's pantheon of greats. His impact on the club's global profile and his role in modernizing the Premier League were also widely acknowledged.

However, there were also those who felt that Wenger's later years had tarnished his legacy. The long trophy drought between 2005 and 2014, the repeated failures to challenge for the Premier League title, and the club's struggles in Europe led some to question whether Wenger had stayed at the helm for too long. The growing disconnect between

Wenger and sections of the fanbase during his final years was a source of tension, and for some, the end of his tenure came as a relief.

Ultimately, Wenger's legacy is a complex and multifaceted one. While the final years were marked by challenges and disappointments, they do not diminish the immense contributions he made to Arsenal and to football. Wenger's influence on the game, his visionary approach, and his unwavering commitment to his principles have left an indelible mark on the sport.

As Arsenal prepared to move into a new chapter without Wenger, there was a sense of both loss and anticipation. The club faced the daunting task of replacing a figure who had been its guiding force for over two decades. Yet, there was also hope that a new era could bring renewed success and that Wenger's legacy would provide a strong foundation for the future.

In the years that followed, Wenger's impact would continue to be felt, not only at Arsenal but across the world of football. His tenure at Arsenal remains one of the most significant chapters in the history of the club, and his legacy as a pioneer, a mentor, and a champion of beautiful football endures.

Chapter 25: The Unai Emery Era (2018-2019)

A New Beginning: Emery's Appointment and the Expectations

In the summer of 2018, Arsenal embarked on a new chapter in their history with the appointment of Unai Emery as the club's head coach. Emery was chosen to succeed Arsène Wenger, whose 22-year tenure had come to an emotional end. The decision to hire Emery marked a significant shift for Arsenal, as the club sought to move away from the Wenger era and embrace a new direction.

Emery arrived at Arsenal with an impressive resume, having won three consecutive Europa League titles with Sevilla and a domestic treble with Paris Saint-Germain. His reputation as a tactician and his experience in European competitions made him an appealing choice for Arsenal, who were looking to return to the upper echelons of English and European football.

The expectations surrounding Emery's appointment were high. Arsenal fans and the board hoped that he would bring a fresh perspective and reinvigorate a team that had struggled in Wenger's final years. Emery was seen as a manager who could introduce a more pragmatic approach, focusing on defensive organization and tactical discipline, areas where Arsenal had been found wanting in recent seasons.

Emery's task was daunting. He needed to manage the transition from the Wenger era, implement his own philosophy, and get the best out of a squad that had underperformed in recent years. The club's failure to qualify for the Champions League for two consecutive seasons added to the pressure, as there was a strong desire to return to Europe's premier competition.

First Season Review: Progress in the League and the Europa League Final Defeat

Emery's first season in charge of Arsenal, the 2018-2019 campaign, was a mix of promise and disappointment. The season began with optimism, as Arsenal went on a 22-match unbeaten run in all competitions, showcasing some of the tactical changes Emery had introduced. The team appeared more organized defensively, and Emery's focus on pressing and intensity in midfield was evident.

In the Premier League, Arsenal were in the hunt for a top-four finish for much of the season. Emery's ability to adapt his tactics to different opponents was praised, and players like Pierre-Emerick Aubameyang, Alexandre Lacazette, and Lucas Torreira thrived under his management. However, inconsistency in the latter part of the season saw Arsenal miss out on a top-four spot by just one point, finishing fifth in the league.

Arsenal's Europa League campaign was a major focus for Emery, given his track record in the competition and the club's desire to secure a return to the Champions League. The Gunners progressed to the final, defeating strong opponents like Napoli and Valencia along the way. The final, held in Baku, saw Arsenal face Chelsea in an all-English affair.

The Europa League final, however, ended in disappointment for Arsenal. Despite a strong first half, Arsenal capitulated in the second half, losing 4-1 to Chelsea. The defeat not only cost Arsenal a European trophy but also denied them a return to the Champions League, a major blow for the club's ambitions. The result was a stark reminder of the challenges Arsenal still faced under Emery, particularly in high-stakes matches.

Challenges and Departure: Struggles in the Second Season Leading to Emery's Sacking

The 2019-2020 season began with hopes that Unai Emery could build on the progress made in his first year and guide Arsenal back into the Champions League. However, the season quickly unraveled, as the team's form deteriorated, and the issues that had plagued Arsenal in the past resurfaced.

Arsenal struggled for consistency, both in the Premier League and in Europe. Defensive frailties, lack of cohesion in midfield, and an inability to control games became recurring themes. Emery's tactical tinkering, which had been seen as a strength in his first season, now appeared to contribute to the team's instability. The frequent changes in formation and personnel left the squad looking disjointed and uncertain.

The atmosphere around the club grew increasingly toxic, with fans becoming frustrated by the lack of progress and the team's poor performances. A series of disappointing results, including a 2-2 draw at home to Crystal Palace after leading 2-0 and a 2-1 loss to Eintracht Frankfurt in the Europa League, piled pressure on Emery.

The breaking point came in November 2019, after a 2-1 defeat at home to Eintracht Frankfurt, which extended Arsenal's winless run to seven games. The result left Arsenal in eighth place in the Premier League and struggling in the Europa League group stage. On November 29, 2019, Arsenal made the decision to part ways with Emery, bringing an end to his tenure after just 18 months.

Emery's departure was met with a mix of relief and regret. While his tenure had shown promise, particularly in his first season, the second season's struggles highlighted the challenges of managing a club in transition. Emery's inability to impose a clear identity on the team and the growing disconnect with the players and fans ultimately led to his downfall.

The end of the Emery era left Arsenal searching for a new direction. The club needed a manager who could not only stabilize the team but also rebuild and restore the club's fortunes. Emery's tenure, though brief, served as a reminder of the complexities involved in succeeding a long-serving manager like Wenger and the importance of finding the right leadership to guide the club forward.

Chapter 26: The Mikel Arteta Project Begins (2019-2020)

Arteta's Arrival: The Return of a Former Player as Manager and His Initial Impact

Following the departure of Unai Emery, Arsenal turned to a familiar face to lead the club into a new era. On December 20, 2019, Mikel Arteta, a former Arsenal captain and then-assistant coach at Manchester City, was appointed as the new head coach. Arteta, who had spent five years at Arsenal as a player, was seen as a promising young manager with the potential to restore the club's fortunes.

Arteta's appointment was met with cautious optimism. Although he lacked managerial experience, having never been a head coach before, Arteta had learned under one of the best in the business—Pep Guardiola. His time at Manchester City had given him a deep understanding of modern football tactics and the demands of managing at the highest level. Moreover, his connection to Arsenal and his understanding of the club's culture endeared him to the fans.

Arteta's initial impact was evident in the way he began to address the team's weaknesses. He focused on improving Arsenal's defensive structure, something that had been a major issue under both Wenger and Emery. Arteta introduced a more organized and disciplined approach, emphasizing the importance of shape, pressing, and defensive responsibility. He also sought to instill a winning mentality and a sense of accountability within the squad.

One of Arteta's early successes was his ability to rejuvenate players who had struggled under Emery. Granit Xhaka, who had been stripped of the captaincy after a public fallout with the fans, was given a new lease on life under Arteta and became a key figure in the midfield. Similarly, David Luiz, who had been error-prone in the previous regime, found stability and form under Arteta's guidance.

Arteta also placed a strong emphasis on team spirit and unity. He worked to create a positive atmosphere within the squad, encouraging a sense of togetherness and collective responsibility. This approach began to pay dividends, as Arsenal's performances improved, and the team started to show signs of progress.

Stabilizing the Team: Early Results, Tactical Changes, and Building Team Spirit

Arteta's arrival brought a sense of stability to Arsenal, both on and off the pitch. The early results under his management were promising, with the team displaying greater defensive solidity and a clearer tactical identity. Arteta implemented a 4-2-3-1 formation, which provided balance between defense and attack, and allowed Arsenal to control games more effectively.

One of the key tactical changes Arteta made was the introduction of a more structured pressing system. He emphasized the importance of winning the ball high up the pitch and transitioning quickly into attack. This approach suited Arsenal's forwards, particularly Pierre-Emerick Aubameyang and Alexandre Lacazette, who thrived in the new system.

Arteta also focused on improving Arsenal's build-up play from the back. He encouraged his defenders and midfielders to play out from the back with composure, creating opportunities to progress the ball through the lines. This approach required confidence and technical ability, and while there were initial teething problems, the team gradually became more comfortable with the new style.

Building team spirit was another cornerstone of Arteta's project. He made it clear that every player had a role to play and that individual success would be achieved through collective effort. Arteta's leadership and communication skills were praised by the players, who responded positively to his methods. The sense of unity within the squad was reflected in their performances, particularly in tough matches where Arsenal showed resilience and determination.

Arteta's focus on discipline and work ethic also extended to his selection policy. He made bold decisions, such as dropping high-profile players who did not meet his standards, and promoting young talents like Bukayo Saka and Gabriel Martinelli, who quickly became integral to the team. Arteta's willingness to give opportunities to young players resonated with the fans and demonstrated his commitment to building a team for the future.

The 2020 FA Cup Victory: The Significance of Winning a Trophy in Arteta's First Season

The crowning achievement of Mikel Arteta's first season in charge of Arsenal was the 2020 FA Cup victory. Winning the FA Cup was a significant milestone for Arteta, as it not only provided tangible success but also validated his methods and philosophy at a time when the club was undergoing a period of transition.

Arsenal's path to the FA Cup final was marked by impressive performances against some of the best teams in English football. In the semifinals, Arsenal faced Manchester City, the team Arteta had left to join Arsenal just months earlier. In a tactical masterclass, Arteta's Arsenal nullified City's attacking threat and secured a 2-0 victory, with Aubameyang scoring both goals. The result was a statement of intent from Arteta and his team, showcasing their ability to compete with and defeat top opposition.

The final, played on August 1, 2020, saw Arsenal face Chelsea in a rematch of the 2017 FA Cup final. The match began poorly for Arsenal, as Christian Pulisic gave Chelsea an early lead. However, Arsenal responded with character and composure. Aubameyang, who had been in sensational form throughout the competition, equalized from the penalty spot before scoring a brilliant second goal in the 67th minute to secure a 2-1 victory.

The FA Cup triumph was a moment of immense pride for Arsenal and for Arteta personally. It marked the club's 14th FA Cup victory, extending their record as the most successful club in the competition's history. For Arteta, winning a major trophy in his first season as a head coach was a remarkable achievement and provided a solid foundation upon which to build his project.

The victory also reinforced the belief within the squad and among the fans that Arsenal were on the right path under Arteta's leadership. It was a testament to the progress made in a short period and offered hope for the future. The FA Cup win not only secured Arsenal's place in the UEFA Europa League for the following season but also demonstrated that the club could still compete for and win major honors.

As Arsenal looked ahead to the 2020-2021 season, the FA Cup victory provided momentum and confidence. Arteta's first season had laid the groundwork for what he hoped would be a successful rebuild, and the trophy was a symbol of the club's resilience and ambition. The challenge now was to build on this success, strengthen the squad, and continue the journey back to the top of English football.

Chapter 27: Building for the Future (2020-2022)

Transfer Strategies: Key Signings and the Emphasis on Young Talent

As Arsenal entered the 2020-2021 season, Mikel Arteta and the club's management recognized the need to reshape the squad and lay the foundation for long-term success. The previous years had seen a mix of expensive signings and inconsistent performances, leading to a realization that a more strategic approach to transfers was necessary. Arteta, along with technical director Edu, implemented a transfer strategy focused on bringing in young, talented players who could develop and grow with the club.

The transfer strategy during this period emphasized both the recruitment of promising young talents and the integration of Arsenal's own academy graduates into the first team. The club's signings reflected this approach, with a focus on players who had the potential to become key figures in the future.

One of the standout signings was the acquisition of Gabriel Magalhães from Lille in the summer of 2020. The young Brazilian center-back quickly established himself as a crucial part of Arsenal's defense, bringing physicality, composure, and leadership to the backline. Gabriel's partnership with the experienced David Luiz, and later with Ben White, provided Arsenal with the defensive solidity that had been lacking in previous seasons.

In the same transfer window, Arsenal secured the services of Thomas Partey from Atlético Madrid. Partey, a powerful and dynamic midfielder, was brought in to add strength and control to Arsenal's midfield. His ability to break up play, drive the ball forward, and contribute defensively made him a key component of Arteta's plans.

Another significant move was the loan signing, and eventual permanent acquisition, of Martin Ødegaard from Real Madrid. The Norwegian playmaker added creativity and vision to Arsenal's midfield, becoming a central figure in Arteta's system. Ødegaard's influence grew over time, and he was later named club captain, highlighting his importance to the team.

Arsenal's transfer strategy also involved promoting young talents from the academy. Bukayo Saka and Emile Smith Rowe, both products of the club's youth system, were given prominent roles in the first team. Saka, in particular, became one of Arsenal's standout performers, showcasing versatility, maturity, and technical ability beyond his years. Smith Rowe, known for his energy and intelligence on the ball, provided a creative spark in midfield and in attacking positions.

The club's emphasis on youth and smart recruitment was a deliberate effort to build a squad capable of competing at the highest level for years to come. Arteta and Edu's strategy focused not only on immediate impact but also on the long-term development of a cohesive and dynamic team.

Developing a New Identity: Arteta's Vision for the Team and Its Playing Style

As Mikel Arteta began to shape his Arsenal side, it became clear that he had a distinct vision for the team's identity and playing style. Arteta's approach was influenced by his time as a player under Arsène Wenger and as an assistant coach under Pep Guardiola at Manchester City. He sought to combine the attacking flair and possession-based football of Wenger's Arsenal with the tactical discipline and intensity of Guardiola's City.

Arteta's vision for Arsenal was centered around three key principles: defensive solidity, controlled possession, and quick transitions. He believed that a strong defense was the foundation of any successful team, and he worked tirelessly to improve Arsenal's defensive structure. The addition of players like Gabriel and Partey, along with the development of existing players, helped Arsenal become more resilient at the back.

In terms of playing style, Arteta encouraged his team to dominate possession and control the tempo of matches. Arsenal's build-up play was characterized by patient passing and movement, with an emphasis on playing out from the back. Arteta wanted his players to be comfortable on the ball, making intelligent decisions and maintaining composure under pressure. This approach required technical proficiency and a high level of tactical awareness, which Arteta instilled through rigorous training and clear instructions.

Arteta also placed a strong emphasis on pressing and counter-pressing. When Arsenal lost the ball, they were expected to win it back quickly, disrupting the opposition's rhythm and creating opportunities to attack in transition. This high-energy style of play suited the younger players in the squad, who brought intensity and enthusiasm to the pitch.

Another important aspect of Arteta's vision was the development of a winning mentality and a strong team spirit. He wanted his players to believe in their abilities and to approach every match with confidence and determination. Arteta's leadership style, characterized by clear communication and a focus on collective responsibility, helped to foster a sense of unity within the squad.

Over time, Arsenal began to show signs of progress, with the team playing with greater coherence and purpose. The new identity that Arteta was building was not without its challenges, but it was clear that the club was moving in a positive direction.

Challenges and Progress: The Ups and Downs of the 2020-21 and 2021-22 Seasons

The 2020-2021 season was a rollercoaster for Arsenal, as the team experienced both highs and lows while adapting to Arteta's methods. The season began with optimism following the FA Cup victory in August 2020, but Arsenal's form in the Premier League was inconsistent. A poor run of results in the first half of the season left the club languishing in the bottom half of the table, raising questions about Arteta's future.

Despite the challenges, Arteta remained committed to his vision and continued to make tactical adjustments. A turning point came during the festive period, when Arsenal secured a crucial 3-1 victory over Chelsea. The introduction of Emile Smith Rowe into the starting lineup injected creativity and energy into the team, and Arsenal's form improved in the second half of the season.

Arsenal's European campaign saw them reach the semifinals of the Europa League, where they faced Villarreal, managed by former Arsenal boss Unai Emery. The two-legged tie ended in disappointment for Arsenal, as they were eliminated after a 2-1 aggregate defeat. The failure to reach the final was a major setback, as it meant Arsenal would miss out on European football for the first time in 25 years.

The 2021-2022 season began with renewed hope, but also with the pressure of returning to European competition. Arsenal's summer transfer window was marked by the acquisition of several young players, including Ben White, Aaron Ramsdale, and Takehiro Tomiyasu. These signings were made with an eye on the future, as Arteta and Edu continued to build a squad that aligned with their long-term vision.

The season started poorly, with Arsenal losing their first three league matches, including a 5-0 defeat to Manchester City. However, Arteta managed to steady the ship, and the team embarked on a strong run of form that saw them climb the table. The emergence of young stars like Bukayo Saka, Emile Smith Rowe, and Gabriel Martinelli provided Arsenal with a fresh impetus, and the team's performances improved significantly.

Arsenal's push for a top-four finish and a return to the Champions League was one of the key storylines of the season. The team remained in contention for much of the campaign, but a series of costly defeats in the final weeks of the season saw them finish fifth, narrowly missing out on Champions League qualification.

Despite the disappointment of missing out on the top four, there were clear signs of progress under Arteta. The team's style of play had evolved, the young players had taken significant strides forward, and the foundations were being laid for future success. The challenges faced during these two seasons were part of the growing pains of a team in transition, but they also highlighted the potential for Arsenal to re-establish themselves as a top force in English football.

Chapter 28: Arsenal's Resurgence (2022-Present)

Youth Revolution: The Rise of Players Like Bukayo Saka, Emile Smith Rowe, and Gabriel Martinelli

The 2022-2023 season marked a period of resurgence for Arsenal, with the club's young talents taking center stage. Bukayo Saka, Emile Smith Rowe, and Gabriel Martinelli emerged as the driving forces behind Arsenal's revival, embodying the youthful energy and attacking flair that Mikel Arteta sought to instill in the team.

Bukayo Saka, who had already established himself as a key player for both Arsenal and the England national team, continued to develop into one of the Premier League's most exciting talents. His versatility, intelligence, and technical ability made him indispensable to Arteta's plans. Saka's ability to play on either wing, as a full-back, or even in midfield gave Arsenal tactical flexibility, and his consistent performances earned him widespread acclaim.

Emile Smith Rowe, known affectionately as the "Croydon De Bruyne" by Arsenal fans, became a central figure in the team's midfield. Smith Rowe's vision, close control, and ability to drive forward with the ball added a new dimension to Arsenal's attack. His knack for scoring crucial goals and his understanding with Saka made them one of the most dynamic young duos in the league. Smith Rowe's rise from academy prospect to first-team regular was a testament to Arteta's belief in nurturing homegrown talent.

Gabriel Martinelli, the Brazilian forward with explosive pace and a keen eye for goal, also played a pivotal role in Arsenal's resurgence. After overcoming injury setbacks, Martinelli returned to the first team with a renewed sense of purpose. His direct style of play, relentless pressing, and ability to score from various positions made him a nightmare for defenders. Martinelli's passion and work ethic endeared him to the Arsenal faithful, and he quickly became a fan favorite.

The contributions of Saka, Smith Rowe, and Martinelli were emblematic of Arsenal's youth revolution under Arteta. The trio, along with other young players like Ben White, Aaron Ramsdale, and Martin Ødegaard, formed the core of a team that was both exciting to watch and capable of challenging for honors. Their rise signaled a bright future for Arsenal and provided a platform for sustained success.

Competing for Titles Again: Arsenal's Renewed Challenge for the Premier League and European Places

As the 2022-2023 season progressed, it became clear that Arsenal were once again a force to be reckoned with in the Premier League. The team's consistent performances, particularly against top opposition, signaled that Arsenal were serious contenders for a top-four finish and, potentially, a Premier League title challenge.

Arteta's tactical approach, which emphasized high pressing, quick transitions, and controlled possession, had begun to take full effect. Arsenal's defense, anchored by the likes of Gabriel Magalhães, Ben White, and the impressive Aaron Ramsdale in goal, was solid and difficult to break down. The midfield, orchestrated by Martin Ødegaard and supported by the industrious Thomas Partey, provided the platform for Arsenal's attacking players to flourish.

The team's attacking prowess was on full display throughout the season, with Saka, Martinelli, and Ødegaard leading the charge. Arsenal's ability to score goals from multiple sources made them one of the most dangerous teams in the league. The addition of Gabriel Jesus, signed from Manchester

City in the summer of 2022, added further firepower and experience to the squad.

Arsenal's progress in the Premier League was mirrored by their performances in European competitions. After a period of absence from the Champions League, Arsenal's return to European football saw them competing in the UEFA Europa League, with the aim of going deep into the competition and securing silverware.

As the season reached its climax, Arsenal found themselves in the mix for both domestic and European honors. The team's resilience, combined with the tactical acumen of Arteta, had put them in a strong position to challenge for major trophies. The fans, reinvigorated by the team's resurgence, began to believe that Arsenal could once again compete with the best in England and Europe.

Arteta's Leadership: Evaluating Arteta's Management Style and Long-Term Plans

Mikel Arteta's leadership at Arsenal had evolved significantly since his appointment in 2019. His management style, characterized by a blend of tactical intelligence, attention to detail, and strong communication, had transformed Arsenal into a team capable of competing at the highest level.

Arteta's emphasis on discipline and work ethic was evident in the way the team approached each match. He demanded the highest standards from his players, both on and off the pitch, and was not afraid to make tough decisions when necessary. This included sidelining high-profile players who did not meet his expectations, a move that reinforced his authority and earned him the respect of the squad.

Tactically, Arteta had developed a clear identity for his Arsenal team. His focus on playing out from the back, maintaining possession, and pressing aggressively had given Arsenal a distinct style of play. Arteta's ability to adapt his tactics to different opponents and in-game situations also demonstrated his growing maturity as a manager.

Arteta's long-term vision for Arsenal was centered around building a team that could consistently compete for titles. His focus on youth development, combined with smart recruitment, was designed to create a squad with both immediate impact and long-term potential. Arteta was committed to creating a culture of excellence at Arsenal, where every player understood their role and contributed to the team's collective success.

Arteta's leadership was also marked by his ability to connect with the fans. His understanding of Arsenal's history and values, combined with his clear communication and passion for the club, resonated with supporters. Arteta's willingness to engage with the fanbase and his commitment to transparency helped to foster a positive relationship between the manager and the Arsenal faithful.

Looking Forward: The Future Prospects of Arsenal Under Arteta

As Arsenal looked to the future under Mikel Arteta, there was a sense of optimism and anticipation. The progress made during the 2020-2022 period had laid a strong foundation for continued success, and the potential for further growth was evident.

Arteta's vision for Arsenal was one of sustained excellence, where the club would consistently challenge for Premier League titles and compete in the Champions League. The focus on youth development and strategic recruitment meant that Arsenal were building a squad capable of competing at the highest level for years to come.

The rise of players like Bukayo Saka, Emile Smith Rowe, and Gabriel Martinelli was just the beginning. Arsenal's academy continued to produce talented prospects, and Arteta was committed to integrating these young players into the first team. The club's investment in scouting and analytics also ensured that Arsenal remained at the forefront of modern football, capable of identifying and acquiring top talent.

Arteta's leadership, combined with the support of the club's management, provided a stable and ambitious framework for the future. The challenges that lay ahead, including competing against well-funded rivals and navigating the demands of multiple competitions, were significant. However, the progress made under Arteta's stewardship gave Arsenal fans reason to believe that the club was on the path to reclaiming its place among the elite of European football.

Looking forward, Arsenal's prospects were bright. The foundations had been laid, the identity was clear, and the potential for success was tangible. As the club continued to build under Arteta's guidance, the future promised to be an exciting and rewarding journey for Arsenal and its supporters.

Chapter 29: The Foundation of Arsenal Women (1987-1992)

Creation of the Team: The Establishment of Arsenal Women and Their Early Struggles

The story of Arsenal Women begins in 1987, a pivotal year for the club and women's football in England. Arsenal Women was founded by Vic Akers, who was also a part of the backroom staff of Arsenal's men's team. Akers, with a deep passion for football and a vision for the future of the women's game, took it upon himself to establish a women's team at Arsenal—a bold move at a time when women's football was still in its infancy in the UK.

The early days were challenging. The team started with limited resources, and women's football did not enjoy the same level of support or infrastructure that men's football had. Arsenal Women, like many other women's teams of the era, faced issues such as lack of funding, poor facilities, and limited media coverage. The players, many of whom were amateurs with full-time jobs, had to balance their professional lives with their passion for football.

Despite these challenges, Akers' dedication and vision began to bear fruit. He recruited players who shared his enthusiasm and commitment, and together they began to lay the foundations for what would become one of the most successful women's football teams in history. The team started competing in regional leagues, where they quickly made a name for themselves with their skill and determination.

The early struggles also fostered a strong sense of camaraderie and resilience within the squad. The players were driven not only by a love of the game but also by a desire to break down barriers and prove that women's football could thrive. This determination would become a hallmark of Arsenal Women as they began to grow and achieve success in the years to come.

First Successes: The Team's Early Triumphs in Domestic Competitions

The hard work and perseverance of Arsenal Women soon started to pay off. The team's first taste of success came in the 1991-1992 season, just five years after their formation. Arsenal Women won the Women's FA Cup, the most prestigious domestic cup competition in English women's football. The victory was a significant milestone for the team and a testament to the progress they had made under Vic Akers' leadership.

The 1991-1992 FA Cup final was held at Prenton Park, and Arsenal faced a strong Southampton

Women's team, which had dominated the competition in previous years. Arsenal, however, showed no signs of intimidation. They played with confidence and skill, ultimately securing a 1-0 victory, with Karen Matthews scoring the decisive goal. The triumph marked Arsenal Women's arrival on the national stage and was the first of many successes to come.

Following their FA Cup victory, Arsenal Women continued to build on their momentum. The team's early successes were not limited to cup competitions; they also began to make their mark in league play. In the 1992-1993 season, Arsenal won the National League Cup, adding another trophy to their growing collection. The team's ability to compete at the highest level of women's football in England was becoming increasingly evident.

These early triumphs laid the groundwork for Arsenal Women's future dominance. The victories in the FA Cup and National League Cup gave the team a taste of success and the belief that they could achieve even greater things. The early 1990s were a period of growth and consolidation for Arsenal Women, as they began to establish themselves as a force in English women's football.

Chapter 30: Dominance in Women's Football (1993-2007)

National and International Success: Arsenal Women's Domination in England and Europe

The period from 1993 to 2007 was one of unprecedented success for Arsenal Women, as they established themselves as the dominant force in English women's football and began to make their mark on the European stage. Under the continued leadership of Vic Akers, Arsenal Women set new standards of excellence and became a symbol of the potential and growth of women's football.

Domestically, Arsenal Women were virtually unstoppable. The team won their first Women's Premier League title in 1992-1993 and then went on to win the league title almost every year for the next decade and a half. Their dominance in the league was matched by their success in cup competitions. Between 1993 and 2007, Arsenal Women won the FA Cup multiple times, often doing so in style, with commanding performances in the finals.

Arsenal's domestic success was not limited to the league and FA Cup. The team also excelled in the League Cup, winning it on numerous occasions during this period. The consistency with which Arsenal Women collected silverware was remarkable, and they became the standard-bearers for women's football in England.

Arsenal's dominance extended beyond England as they began to make significant strides in European competitions. The pinnacle of their success came in the 2006-2007 season when Arsenal Women became the first English club to win the UEFA Women's Cup, the premier club competition in European women's football (now known as the UEFA Women's Champions League).

Key Figures: Profiles of Influential Players and Managers

Arsenal Women's success during this period was built on the contributions of several key figures, both on and off the pitch. Vic Akers, the team's manager, was the driving force behind the club's rise to prominence. His vision, dedication, and tactical acumen were instrumental in building a team capable of dominating at both national and international levels. Akers' leadership was characterized by a deep commitment to the development of women's football and the players under his guidance.

Among the standout players during this era was Kelly Smith, widely regarded as one of the greatest female footballers of her generation. Smith's skill, creativity, and goal-scoring ability made her a talismanic figure for Arsenal Women. Her impact on the team's success was immense, and she played a pivotal role in their domestic and European triumphs.

Another influential figure was Faye White, who captained Arsenal Women for many years and was a commanding presence in defense. White's leadership on the pitch, combined with her defensive prowess, helped to establish Arsenal's reputation as a team that was not only brilliant in attack but also rock-solid at the back.

Other notable players included Rachel Yankey, a dynamic winger known for her pace and crossing ability, and Julie Fleeting, a prolific striker who was instrumental in many of Arsenal's victories. These players, along with many others, formed the core of a team that was unparalleled in its success and influence.

The 2007 UEFA Women's Cup Win: Arsenal's Historic European Victory

The crowning achievement of Arsenal Women's dominance during this period was their victory in the 2007 UEFA Women's Cup. The triumph was not only historic for Arsenal but also for English women's football, as it marked the first time that an English club had won the prestigious European title.

Arsenal's journey to the final was a testament to their quality and determination. The team navigated through the group stages and knockout rounds with a series of impressive performances, showcasing their technical ability, tactical discipline, and mental toughness.

In the final, Arsenal faced Swedish side Umeå IK, one of the strongest teams in Europe at the time. The first leg, played in Sweden, ended in a 1-0 victory for Arsenal, with a goal from Alex Scott. The second leg, held at Borehamwood's Meadow Park, was a tense and closely contested affair. Arsenal's defense, led by Faye White and supported by goalkeeper Emma Byrne, held firm, and the match ended in a 0-0 draw. Arsenal's 1-0 aggregate victory secured the UEFA Women's Cup, a landmark achievement in the club's history.

The 2007 UEFA Women's Cup win was a moment of immense pride for Arsenal Women and a recognition of their dominance in the sport. It solidified their status as one of the best teams in Europe and demonstrated the strength of women's football in England. The victory also highlighted the contributions of Vic Akers and his players, who had worked tirelessly to reach the pinnacle of European football.

Chapter 31: Arsenal Women in the Modern Era (2008-Present)

Competing in the WSL: The Team's Performance in the FA Women's Super League

The introduction of the FA Women's Super League (WSL) in 2011 marked a new chapter in the history of women's football in England, and Arsenal Women were at the forefront of this new era. As one of the most successful and established teams in the country, Arsenal entered the WSL with high expectations and continued to be a dominant force.

Arsenal Women won the inaugural WSL title in 2011, demonstrating their continued excellence and adaptability in a rapidly evolving landscape. The team's success in the WSL was built on the foundation laid by Vic Akers and carried forward by subsequent managers. Arsenal's style of play, characterized by technical skill, fluid movement, and a strong team ethic, allowed them to compete at the highest level.

Throughout the 2010s, Arsenal remained one of the top teams in the WSL, consistently finishing near the top of the table and competing for domestic honors. The team's performances in the league were complemented by their success in cup competitions, including multiple FA Cup and League Cup victories.

The WSL also brought increased visibility and professionalism to women's football in England, with more media coverage, sponsorship, and investment in the women's game. Arsenal Women benefited from these developments, attracting top talent from around the world and continuing to build on their legacy of success.

Impact of Professionalization: The Effect of Increased Investment and Professionalism in Women's Football

The professionalization of women's football, particularly with the advent of the WSL, had a profound impact on Arsenal Women and the broader landscape of the sport. Increased investment from the club and greater support from sponsors and broadcasters helped to raise the profile of the team and provided the resources needed to compete at the highest level.

The professionalization of the game also led to improvements in training facilities, coaching, and player development. Arsenal Women benefited from access to state-of-the-art facilities and the expertise of top coaches, which helped to enhance the performance and development of the players.

The increased professionalism also attracted more international talent to the WSL, raising the standard of competition and providing Arsenal Women with the opportunity to compete against some of the best players in the world. This influx of talent, combined with the club's commitment to nurturing homegrown players, created a strong and competitive squad capable of challenging for titles both domestically and in Europe.

However, the professionalization of the game also brought new challenges. The increased competition in the WSL meant that Arsenal Women faced tougher opposition, and maintaining their position at the top of the league required continuous improvement and adaptation. The financial backing of rival clubs also intensified the competition for top players, making it essential for Arsenal to continue investing in their team and infrastructure.

Continued Success: Recent Triumphs and Key Players of the Current Era

Despite the challenges of an increasingly competitive landscape, Arsenal Women continued to enjoy success in the modern era. The team's commitment to excellence and their ability to adapt to the evolving demands of the sport allowed them to remain a force in English and European football.

In the 2018-2019 season, Arsenal Women won their first WSL title since 2012, under the management of Joe Montemurro. The team's title-winning campaign was marked by a combination of attacking brilliance and defensive solidity. Players like Vivianne Miedema, the league's top scorer, were instrumental in Arsenal's success, while Leah Williamson and Jordan Nobbs provided leadership and stability in defense and midfield, respectively.

Arsenal Women's success in the WSL was complemented by strong performances in cup competitions. The team continued to compete for and win the FA Cup and League Cup, adding to their already impressive trophy cabinet. The club's ability to consistently challenge for honors was a testament to the strength of their squad and the effectiveness of their management.

Key players of the modern era, such as Vivianne Miedema, have continued to elevate Arsenal Women's status on the global stage. Miedema, known for her clinical finishing and intelligent movement, has been one of the standout performers in the WSL and has broken numerous goal-scoring records. Her contributions, along with those of players like Kim Little, Danielle van de Donk, and Beth Mead, have ensured that Arsenal Women remain competitive at the highest level.

The recent years have also seen a renewed focus on youth development, with Arsenal Women's academy producing talented players who have gone on to make significant contributions to the first team. The integration of young talent into the senior squad has been a key aspect of the club's strategy, ensuring that Arsenal Women continue to build for the future.

As Arsenal Women look ahead, the club remains committed to maintaining its legacy of success and continuing to be a leader in women's football. The challenges of competing in an increasingly professional and competitive environment are significant, but the foundations laid over the past three decades provide a strong platform for future success. The combination of experienced international stars and emerging young talent ensures that Arsenal Women will remain a formidable force in the years to come, both in England and on the European stage.

Chapter 32: Community and Charity Work

Local Impact: Arsenal's Role in the North London Community

Arsenal Football Club has always recognized its deep roots in the North London community and has long been committed to making a positive impact on the local area. Since its early days, Arsenal has been more than just a football club; it has been a pillar of the community, actively engaging with local residents, schools, and organizations to improve lives and foster a sense of belonging.

The club's local impact is most evident through its numerous community outreach programs. Arsenal in the Community, established in 1985, has played a pivotal role in this effort. The program focuses on using the power of football to inspire and support people across North London. Arsenal in the Community runs a variety of initiatives aimed at promoting education, physical activity, social inclusion, and health and well-being.

One of the key aspects of Arsenal's local impact has been its work in education. The club has partnered with local schools to deliver educational programs that use football as a tool to engage students and encourage learning. These programs cover a wide range of subjects, including literacy, numeracy, and life skills, helping to motivate young people and provide them with valuable opportunities.

Arsenal has also been instrumental in promoting physical health and well-being in the community. The club's sports programs, including football coaching sessions and fitness classes, are designed to encourage active lifestyles and provide a safe and inclusive environment for people of all ages to stay fit and healthy. These programs often target underrepresented groups, including women, girls, and individuals with disabilities, ensuring that everyone in the community has the chance to participate.

Social inclusion is another key focus of Arsenal's community work. The club has implemented various initiatives aimed at bringing people together and breaking down barriers, whether related to race, gender, or economic background. Through workshops, events, and outreach activities, Arsenal has helped to foster a sense of unity and inclusion in North London, using football as a common language that transcends differences.

Global Initiatives: The Club's Involvement in Global Charity Projects

While Arsenal's roots are firmly planted in North London, the club's influence and commitment to making a difference extend far beyond the UK. Arsenal has become increasingly involved in global charity projects, using its platform to support communities in need around the world.

One of the key ways Arsenal has contributed globally is through partnerships with international charities and organizations. The club has supported initiatives that address a wide range of issues, including poverty, education, health, and disaster relief. Arsenal's involvement in these projects has helped to raise awareness and provide much-needed resources to those affected by crises and challenges.

For example, Arsenal has partnered with Save the Children, a global organization dedicated to improving the lives of children in the world's most vulnerable communities. Through this partnership, Arsenal has supported education programs, emergency response efforts, and initiatives aimed at protecting children's rights. The club's support has included fundraising campaigns, player appearances, and donations, all aimed at making a positive impact on the lives of children worldwide.

Arsenal has also been involved in projects that promote sport as a tool for development and peace. The club has supported initiatives that use football to bring communities together, promote social cohesion, and provide opportunities for young people in regions affected by conflict and poverty. These projects often focus on empowering young people through sport, giving them the skills, confidence, and hope they need to build better futures.

The global reach of Arsenal's charity work reflects the club's commitment to being a force for good in the world. By leveraging its global brand and influence, Arsenal has been able to make a difference in the lives of people far beyond its North London base, demonstrating that football can be a powerful tool for positive change on a global scale.

The Arsenal Foundation: The Work and Achievements of the Club's Charity Arm

The Arsenal Foundation, established in 2012, serves as the charitable arm of Arsenal Football Club. Its mission is to support young people and local communities through a range of initiatives that harness the power of football to inspire and empower. The Foundation's work is deeply rooted in the values of the club, focusing on education, social inclusion, and community cohesion.

One of the key achievements of the Arsenal Foundation has been its commitment to supporting education and opportunities for young people. The

Foundation funds a variety of programs that aim to improve educational outcomes, provide life skills training, and create pathways to employment. These programs are designed to give young people the tools they need to succeed, both on and off the pitch.

The Foundation's work in the area of social inclusion is also noteworthy. Through its support of initiatives that promote diversity, equality, and inclusion, the Arsenal Foundation has helped to create a more inclusive environment both within football and in the wider community. This includes funding for programs that address issues such as racism, discrimination, and social isolation, as well as initiatives that promote the inclusion of underrepresented groups in sport.

In addition to its work in North London, the Arsenal Foundation has also supported projects with a global impact. This includes funding for initiatives that provide education, health care, and emergency relief in some of the world's most disadvantaged communities. The Foundation's global projects often focus on using football as a tool for development, helping to bring hope and opportunity to young people in challenging circumstances.

One of the most visible aspects of the Arsenal Foundation's work is its fundraising efforts. The

Foundation organizes a variety of events and campaigns to raise money for its projects, often involving players, staff, and supporters. These efforts have raised millions of pounds for charity and have made a significant difference in the lives of countless individuals and communities.

The Arsenal Foundation's achievements are a testament to the club's commitment to giving back and making a positive impact on the world. Through its support of education, social inclusion, and community development, the Foundation embodies the values of Arsenal Football Club and serves as a powerful example of how sport can be a force for good.

Chapter 33: Arsenal's Global Fanbase

The Globalization of Arsenal: The Club's Expansion Beyond the UK

Over the years, Arsenal Football Club has grown from a local team in North London to a global sporting brand with a fanbase that spans every corner of the world. The globalization of Arsenal has been driven by the club's success on the pitch, its commitment to playing attractive football, and its ability to connect with fans across cultures and geographies.

Arsenal's global expansion began in earnest during the Arsène Wenger era, particularly in the late 1990s and early 2000s, when the club enjoyed unprecedented success in the Premier League and Europe. Wenger's emphasis on attacking football, combined with the presence of international stars like Thierry Henry, Patrick Vieira, and Dennis Bergkamp, helped to attract a worldwide audience. The club's success, combined with the growing popularity of the Premier League, contributed to Arsenal's burgeoning global following.

The advent of digital media and the internet further accelerated Arsenal's global reach. The club's website, social media channels, and online content have allowed fans from around the world to stay connected with the team, regardless of their location. Arsenal's digital presence has been crucial in building and maintaining a global fanbase, offering supporters access to news, interviews, match highlights, and behind-the-scenes content.

Arsenal has also engaged in international tours and friendly matches, bringing the team to different parts of the world and allowing fans to see their heroes in action. These tours have taken Arsenal to countries such as the United States, China, Australia, and Singapore, where they have played in front of enthusiastic crowds and connected with local communities. The tours have not only expanded Arsenal's global footprint but have also helped to strengthen the bond between the club and its international supporters.

The globalization of Arsenal has also been supported by partnerships with international brands and sponsors, which have helped to enhance the club's visibility and appeal worldwide. These partnerships have included collaborations with companies in sectors such as sportswear, technology, and finance, further embedding Arsenal's brand in global markets.

Supporter Groups Worldwide: The Rise of International Fan Clubs and Their Influence

One of the most significant aspects of Arsenal's global fanbase is the rise of international supporter groups. These fan clubs, located in cities around the world, play a vital role in bringing Arsenal fans together, fostering a sense of community, and supporting the team from afar.

Arsenal's international supporter groups are officially recognized by the club and are an integral part of its global network. These groups organize events, watch parties, and social gatherings, providing fans with the opportunity to connect with fellow Gooners and share their passion for the club. Whether in New York, Lagos, Sydney, or Tokyo, Arsenal fans can find a community of like-minded supporters to watch matches and celebrate the team's successes.

The influence of these supporter groups extends beyond social gatherings. Many of these groups engage in charity work, community outreach, and initiatives that support local causes. By doing so, they not only promote the values of Arsenal Football Club but also make a positive impact in their local communities. This blend of fandom and philanthropy reflects the ethos of Arsenal and strengthens the connection between the club and its supporters.

The rise of international fan clubs has also had an impact on how Arsenal communicates with its global audience. The club has made efforts to tailor its content and engagement strategies to different regions, recognizing the diverse cultural backgrounds of its fans. This has included offering content in multiple languages, creating region-specific social media accounts, and engaging with fan clubs directly to ensure that their voices are heard.

The passion and dedication of Arsenal's international supporter groups have made them a vital part of the club's identity. Their influence can be seen in the global reach of Arsenal's brand, the atmosphere at international matches, and the sense of unity that transcends borders.

Famous Fans: Notable Celebrities and Public Figures Who Support Arsenal

Arsenal Football Club has a rich history of attracting high-profile fans from the worlds of entertainment, politics, and sports. These famous supporters have helped to raise the club's profile and bring attention to Arsenal's success on and off the pitch.

One of the most well-known Arsenal fans is Hollywood actor Idris Elba. Elba, who grew up in East London, has been a lifelong supporter of the Gunners and has often spoken about his love for the club. He has been spotted at the Emirates Stadium on several occasions and has even narrated promotional videos for the club.

Another prominent Arsenal fan is musician and songwriter Rod Stewart. Although Stewart is Scottish by birth, he developed a love for Arsenal during his time in London and has been a dedicated supporter for many years. Stewart's passion for the club is well-known, and he has often attended matches and expressed his support publicly.

In the world of sports, Arsenal has attracted fans from various disciplines. Tennis legend Roger Federer has been linked with Arsenal, with reports suggesting that he has a soft spot for the club. Although Federer's primary focus has been tennis, his admiration for Arsenal reflects the club's appeal to athletes across different sports.

In the political sphere, former British Prime Minister Tony Blair is known to have supported Arsenal during his time in office. Blair's connection to the club added a layer of intrigue to his political career, with the media occasionally referencing his support for the Gunners.

Arsenal's global fanbase also includes influential figures such as former basketball star LeBron James, who has shown an interest in the club through social media. LeBron's global reach as an athlete has introduced Arsenal to a broader audience, particularly in the United States.

These famous fans, along with many others, have played a role in enhancing Arsenal's cultural presence and influence. Their support has brought attention to the club in various sectors, contributing to Arsenal's reputation as one of the most popular and respected football clubs in the world.

Chapter 34: Arsenal in Popular Culture

Appearances in Media: Arsenal's Presence in Film, Television, and Literature

Arsenal Football Club's rich history and iconic status have made it a popular subject in various forms of media, including film, television, and literature. The club's influence on popular culture is evident in the numerous references, portrayals, and stories that have featured Arsenal over the years.

One of the most famous depictions of Arsenal in film is the 1997 movie "Fever Pitch," based on the book by Nick Hornby. The film, which stars Colin Firth, tells the story of a man whose life is intertwined with his obsession with Arsenal. "Fever Pitch" is a love letter to the highs and lows of being a football fan, capturing the emotional rollercoaster that comes with supporting a club like Arsenal. The film's depiction of the 1988-89 season, culminating in Arsenal's dramatic title win at Anfield, has become a cultural touchstone for many Arsenal supporters.

Arsenal has also appeared in various television shows, often as a reference point for characters who are fans of the club. In the popular British sitcom "The IT Crowd," one of the main characters, Roy, is a devoted Arsenal fan, and the club is frequently mentioned throughout the series. Similarly, in the

BBC drama "Hustle," one of the main characters, Mickey Bricks, is portrayed as an Arsenal supporter, adding an element of the club's identity to his character.

In literature, Arsenal has been featured in numerous books, both fiction and non-fiction. Nick Hornby's "Fever Pitch" remains one of the most celebrated works about football fandom, offering a deep and personal exploration of what it means to support Arsenal. The book has resonated with football fans around the world and has become a classic in the genre of sports literature.

Arsenal's presence in media extends to documentaries and sports programs that explore the club's history, achievements, and impact. These productions often highlight key moments in Arsenal's history, such as the Invincibles season, the move to the Emirates Stadium, and the legacy of Arsène Wenger. The club's storied past provides rich material for filmmakers and writers, ensuring that Arsenal remains a prominent subject in popular culture.

Music and the Arts: How the Club Has Inspired Musicians, Artists, and Writers

Arsenal's influence extends beyond the realms of sport and media into the world of music and the arts.

The club's history, identity, and culture have inspired musicians, artists, and writers to create works that celebrate and reflect their passion for the Gunners.

One of the most famous musical tributes to Arsenal is the song "Good Old Arsenal," recorded by the team in 1971 to celebrate their FA Cup victory. The song, which became a fan favorite, captures the spirit of the club and has been sung by supporters for decades. The track remains a cherished part of Arsenal's musical legacy and is often played at the Emirates Stadium on matchdays.

Musicians who are Arsenal fans have also paid tribute to the club in their work. The band The Libertines, whose members include devoted Arsenal supporters, have referenced the club in their lyrics and interviews. Similarly, the rapper and grime artist Lethal Bizzle, an outspoken Arsenal fan, has incorporated references to the club in his music and social media presence.

In the visual arts, Arsenal has been the subject of numerous paintings, illustrations, and graphic designs. Artists have captured iconic moments from the club's history, such as Thierry Henry's legendary goal celebrations, the Invincibles lifting the Premier League trophy, and the historic Highbury stadium. These works of art celebrate

Arsenal's legacy and provide a visual representation of the club's impact on its fans and the wider culture.

Writers, too, have been inspired by Arsenal, producing essays, memoirs, and stories that explore the emotional connection between the club and its supporters. The themes of loyalty, passion, and community that are central to football are often explored through the lens of Arsenal, reflecting the deep bond that fans have with the club.

Cultural Impact: Arsenal's Role in Shaping Cultural Trends and Popular Opinion

Arsenal Football Club has played a significant role in shaping cultural trends and popular opinion, both within the world of football and beyond. The club's influence can be seen in the way it has set standards for excellence, innovation, and social responsibility.

One of the most notable examples of Arsenal's cultural impact is the way the club, under Arsène Wenger, revolutionized football in England. Wenger's introduction of new training methods, dietary practices, and a focus on technical skill helped to transform the Premier League and set a new standard for professional football. Arsenal's success during this period, particularly the

Invincibles season, cemented the club's reputation as a pioneer in modern football.

Arsenal has also been at the forefront of promoting diversity and inclusion in football. The club's efforts to combat racism, support LGBTQ+ rights, and promote gender equality have made it a leader in the movement for social justice in sport. Arsenal's "No Room for Racism" campaign and its support for initiatives like Stonewall's Rainbow Laces campaign reflect the club's commitment to using its platform to drive positive change.

The cultural impact of Arsenal extends to fashion and lifestyle, with the club's iconic red and white kit becoming a symbol of style and identity for fans around the world. Arsenal's partnerships with sportswear brands, including Adidas and Nike, have produced some of the most recognizable and beloved football kits in history. These designs have transcended the sport, influencing streetwear and popular fashion trends.

Arsenal's influence on popular opinion is also evident in the way the club is perceived by the public. The values of Arsenal—tradition, innovation, community, and excellence—resonate with fans and non-fans alike. The club's commitment to playing attractive football, its history of success, and its engagement with social issues have made Arsenal one of the most respected and admired football clubs globally.

In conclusion, Arsenal Football Club's presence in popular culture is a reflection of its enduring legacy and its ability to connect with people across different walks of life. Whether through film, music, art, or social impact, Arsenal's influence extends far beyond the pitch, making it a cultural icon in its own right.

Chapter 35: Arsenal's All-Time Legends

Player Profiles: In-Depth Looks at the Most Iconic Players in Arsenal's History

Arsenal Football Club has been home to some of the greatest players in the history of football. These legends have not only left an indelible mark on the club but have also contributed to its storied legacy, inspiring generations of fans and players alike. This chapter delves into the careers and achievements of Arsenal's most iconic players, offering an in-depth look at their contributions to the club.

Thierry Henry

Arguably Arsenal's greatest player of all time, Thierry Henry is synonymous with brilliance. Joining Arsenal in 1999 under Arsène Wenger, Henry quickly established himself as one of the most lethal strikers in world football. Known for his incredible pace, technical skill, and finishing ability, Henry became Arsenal's all-time leading goal scorer with 228 goals across two spells at the club. His role in the Invincibles season, where Arsenal went unbeaten throughout the 2003-2004 Premier League campaign, cemented his status as a legend. Henry's memorable goals, including his iconic strikes against Manchester United and Tottenham

Hotspur, are forever etched in the annals of Arsenal history.

Tony Adams

Tony Adams, affectionately known as "Mr. Arsenal," spent his entire playing career at the club, serving as captain for 14 of his 22 years. A commanding center-back, Adams was the heart and soul of Arsenal's defense, leading the team to numerous titles, including four league championships and three FA Cups. His leadership, loyalty, and tenacity made him a beloved figure among Arsenal fans. Adams' ability to organize the defense and his crucial goals, such as the famous strike against Everton to seal the 1998 Premier League title, highlight his importance to the club.

Dennis Bergkamp

Dennis Bergkamp, the "Non-Flying Dutchman," brought a touch of class and elegance to Arsenal's attack. Joining the club in 1995, Bergkamp's vision, creativity, and technical ability made him one of the most influential players in Arsenal's history. His partnership with Thierry Henry was one of the most potent in Premier League history. Bergkamp's knack for scoring spectacular goals, such as his stunning flick and finish against Newcastle United in 2002, endeared him to Arsenal fans. His contributions were pivotal in Arsenal's success during the late 1990s and early 2000s, including the Double-winning campaigns of 1998 and 2002.

Patrick Vieira

Patrick Vieira was the engine room of Arsenal's midfield during one of the most successful periods in the club's history. Joining Arsenal in 1996, Vieira quickly became known for his physical presence, leadership, and ability to dominate the midfield. As captain, he led the team through the Invincibles season and played a key role in Arsenal's domestic and European success. Vieira's battles with Manchester United's Roy Keane are legendary, and his leadership on the pitch was instrumental in maintaining Arsenal's competitive edge during his time at the club. Vieira's legacy is marked by his contribution to three Premier League titles and four FA Cups.

Ian Wright

Ian Wright was Arsenal's leading goal scorer before Thierry Henry surpassed his record. Known for his infectious enthusiasm and deadly finishing, Wright became a fan favorite during his time at Arsenal. Joining the club in 1991, Wright's goalscoring exploits helped Arsenal win the Premier League title in 1998 and the FA Cup in 1993 and 1998. His record-breaking goal to surpass Cliff Bastin's record as Arsenal's all-time top scorer (later surpassed by Henry) was a testament to his impact on the club. Wright's passion for Arsenal and his goal-scoring prowess have made him one of the club's most beloved figures.

Managers Who Shaped Arsenal: From Chapman to Wenger, A Study of Arsenal's Most Influential Managers

Arsenal's history is marked by the influence of several visionary managers who have shaped the club's identity and success. This section examines the careers and legacies of Arsenal's most influential managers, whose contributions have left a lasting impact on the club.

Herbert Chapman

Herbert Chapman is often regarded as the father of modern Arsenal. Appointed as manager in 1925, Chapman revolutionized English football with his innovative tactics, including the WM formation, and his emphasis on physical fitness and professionalism. Under Chapman's leadership, Arsenal won their first major trophies, including two league titles (1930-31 and 1932-33) and an FA Cup in 1930. Chapman's influence extended beyond the pitch; he was instrumental in the development of

Highbury Stadium, introduced the iconic red-and-white kit, and was a pioneer in using floodlights and numbered shirts. Chapman's untimely death in 1934 cut short his visionary work, but his legacy remains a cornerstone of Arsenal's history.

George Graham

George Graham, known for his emphasis on defensive solidity, managed Arsenal from 1986 to 1995 and led the club to significant success. Under Graham, Arsenal became known for their disciplined defense, famously epitomized by the back four of Dixon, Adams, Bould, and Winterburn. Graham guided Arsenal to two league titles (1988-89 and 1990-91), including the dramatic last-minute victory at Anfield in 1989. He also won the FA Cup, League Cup, and the European Cup Winners' Cup. Despite his controversial departure, Graham's tenure is remembered for instilling a winning mentality and a strong defensive foundation that laid the groundwork for future success.

Arsène Wenger

Arsène Wenger is the longest-serving and most successful manager in Arsenal's history. Appointed in 1996, Wenger revolutionized English football with his emphasis on attacking football, technical excellence, and sports science. Under Wenger,

Arsenal won three Premier League titles, including the iconic Invincibles season in 2003-2004, where the team went unbeaten throughout the league campaign. Wenger also led Arsenal to seven FA Cup victories, making him the most successful manager in the competition's history. Wenger's influence extended beyond the pitch; he oversaw the move to the Emirates Stadium and played a key role in modernizing the club's infrastructure. Wenger's legacy is defined by his commitment to beautiful football, his ability to develop young talent, and his contributions to Arsenal's global identity.

Greatest Matches: An Analysis of the Most Memorable Games in the Club's History

Arsenal's history is filled with memorable matches that have defined the club's legacy and provided unforgettable moments for fans. This section analyzes some of the most iconic games in Arsenal's history, exploring their significance and impact.

Liverpool 0-2 Arsenal (Anfield, 1989) One of the most dramatic moments in English football history, Arsenal's 2-0 victory at Anfield on May 26, 1989, secured the First Division title in the most thrilling fashion. Arsenal needed to win by two clear goals to overtake Liverpool on goal difference and clinch the title. Michael Thomas' last-minute goal sealed the victory, sparking jubilant scenes among Arsenal players and fans. This match is often regarded as one of the greatest in the club's history, symbolizing the resilience and determination of George Graham's Arsenal.

Arsenal 1-0 Parma (Copenhagen, 1994)
The 1994 European Cup Winners' Cup final saw Arsenal take on Parma in Copenhagen. Arsenal, under George Graham, were the underdogs against a strong Parma side featuring players like Gianfranco Zola and Faustino Asprilla. Alan Smith's early goal proved decisive, and Arsenal's disciplined defensive performance ensured a 1-0 victory, securing the club's second major European trophy. This match is remembered for its tactical mastery and the importance of the victory in solidifying Arsenal's status in European football.

Arsenal 2-0 Chelsea (Cardiff, 2002 FA Cup Final)
The 2002 FA Cup final was a key moment in Arsenal's Double-winning season. Facing a strong Chelsea side, Arsenal secured a 2-0 victory with goals from Ray Parlour and Freddie Ljungberg. The win was significant not only for its contribution to the Double but also for the way it showcased Arsenal's attacking flair and resilience. The 2002 Double was a defining achievement for Arsène Wenger's

Arsenal, highlighting the team's dominance in English football at the time.

Arsenal 2-1 Barcelona (Emirates Stadium, 2011)
The 2011 UEFA Champions League Round of 16 first-leg match against Barcelona at the Emirates Stadium is one of Arsenal's most memorable European nights. Arsenal faced a Barcelona side widely regarded as the best in the world, featuring stars like Lionel Messi, Xavi, and Iniesta. Despite going 1-0 down, Arsenal mounted a stunning comeback with goals from Robin van Persie and Andrey Arshavin to secure a 2-1 victory. Although Arsenal were eventually eliminated in the second leg, this match is remembered for the team's resilience, tactical brilliance, and the electric atmosphere at the Emirates.

Chapter 36: Records and Achievements

Club Records: A Compilation of Arsenal's Statistical Records

Arsenal Football Club boasts an impressive array of records that reflect its storied history and success in English and European football. This section compiles some of the most significant records held by the club, highlighting the achievements that have defined Arsenal's legacy.

- **Most League Titles:** Arsenal has won the English top division (First Division/Premier League) 13 times, with their first title coming in the 1930-31 season and their most recent in 2003-2004.

- **Most FA Cup Wins:** Arsenal holds the record for the most FA Cup victories, having won the prestigious competition 14 times, with their first win in 1930 and the most recent in 2020.

- **Most Consecutive Seasons in the Top Flight:** Arsenal holds the record for the most consecutive seasons in the English top flight, having maintained their status in the top division since 1919.

- **Unbeaten League Run:** The 2003-2004 "Invincibles" season saw Arsenal go unbeaten throughout the entire Premier League campaign, a record 38 matches without a loss.

- **Record Transfer Fee (Paid):** Arsenal's record transfer fee was paid for Nicolas Pépé, who joined the club from Lille in 2019 for a reported £72 million.

Season-by-Season Review: A Chronological Summary of Each Season's Key Events and Results

This section provides a comprehensive review of Arsenal's performances across different seasons, offering a chronological summary of key events, results, and achievements. From the early days of the club in the late 19th century to the modern era, this review captures the evolution of Arsenal and the milestones that have defined its history.

Each season's review includes information on league standings, cup runs, key matches, player performances, and managerial changes. The review highlights significant achievements, such as league titles, cup victories, and European campaigns, while also noting challenges and setbacks that the club faced along the way.

This chronological summary serves as a detailed account of Arsenal's journey through the years, offering insights into how the club has grown, adapted, and succeeded in the ever-changing landscape of football.

Rivalries and Memorable Wins: A Focus on Arsenal's Most Heated Rivalries and Significant Victories

Arsenal's history is marked by intense rivalries and memorable victories that have shaped the club's identity and forged its place in football folklore. This section explores some of the most heated rivalries in Arsenal's history and the significant wins that have defined these encounters.

North London Derby: Arsenal vs. Tottenham Hotspur

The North London Derby is one of the fiercest and most storied rivalries in English football. The rivalry between Arsenal and Tottenham Hotspur dates back to 1913 when Arsenal moved to North London. Matches between the two clubs are highly anticipated, with both sets of fans passionately supporting their teams. Memorable wins for Arsenal in this fixture include the 5-4 victory at White Hart Lane in 2004, and the 3-0 win at the Emirates Stadium in 2009, where Cesc Fàbregas scored one of the fastest goals in derby history.

Arsenal vs. Manchester United

The rivalry between Arsenal and Manchester United reached its peak during the late 1990s and early 2000s when both clubs were competing for supremacy in the Premier League. The battles between Arsène Wenger's Arsenal and Sir Alex Ferguson's Manchester United are legendary, with matches often filled with drama, intensity, and high stakes. Significant victories for Arsenal include the 1-0 win at Old Trafford in 2002, where Sylvain Wiltord's goal secured the Premier League title, and the FA Cup semi-final victory in 1999, where Ryan Giggs' memorable goal sent United to the final (despite Arsenal's strong performance).

Arsenal vs. Liverpool

Arsenal's rivalry with Liverpool has produced some of the most memorable matches in English football history. The 1989 title-deciding match at Anfield, where Arsenal won 2-0 to claim the league title, remains one of the most iconic moments in the club's history. The rivalry has continued over the years, with both clubs vying for domestic and European honors.

Arsenal vs. Chelsea

In the modern era, Arsenal's rivalry with Chelsea has intensified, particularly during the 2000s when both clubs were among the top teams in the Premier League. Memorable encounters include Arsenal's 2-0 victory in the 2002 FA Cup final and the 3-2 win at Stamford Bridge in 2011. The rivalry has also seen Chelsea emerge as a strong contender, leading to fierce battles in both the Premier League and domestic cup competitions.

These rivalries and memorable victories have not only defined Arsenal's history but have also contributed to the rich tapestry of English football. The passion, intensity, and significance of these matches continue to captivate fans and add to the enduring legacy of Arsenal Football Club.

Chapter 37: Arsenal's Future

Emerging Talents: Profiles of the Most Promising Young Players

As Arsenal looks toward the future, the development of young talent remains a cornerstone of the club's strategy. The Arsenal academy has a rich history of producing top-tier footballers, and the current crop of emerging talents offers great promise for the club's future success. This section profiles some of the most promising young players who are expected to play pivotal roles in Arsenal's journey ahead.

Bukayo Saka

Bukayo Saka has already established himself as a key player for Arsenal and the England national team, despite his young age. A versatile player capable of excelling as a winger, full-back, or attacking midfielder, Saka's technical ability, vision, and composure on the ball have made him one of the most exciting talents in European football. His maturity and consistency on the pitch, combined with his natural flair, make him a vital part of Arsenal's present and future. Saka's influence on the team is expected to grow even further as he continues to develop and take on more leadership responsibilities.

Emile Smith Rowe

Emile Smith Rowe, known for his creativity and intelligent movement, has become a fan favorite at Arsenal. A product of the club's academy, Smith Rowe's ability to find space and link up play has made him a crucial figure in Mikel Arteta's plans. His knack for scoring important goals and his tireless work rate have earned him the nickname "The Croydon De Bruyne." As Smith Rowe continues to develop his game, he is expected to be a central figure in Arsenal's midfield, driving the team forward with his energy and vision.

Gabriel Martinelli

Gabriel Martinelli, the Brazilian forward, has impressed since his arrival at Arsenal with his pace, tenacity, and eye for goal. Despite battling injuries early in his career, Martinelli has shown flashes of brilliance that suggest he has the potential to become one of Arsenal's leading attackers. His work ethic and determination on the pitch, combined with his ability to play across the front line, make him a valuable asset for the club. As Martinelli gains more experience and consistency, he is expected to play a key role in Arsenal's attacking unit.

Charlie Patino

Charlie Patino is one of the brightest prospects to emerge from Arsenal's academy in recent years. A central midfielder with exceptional technical skills, Patino is known for his composure on the ball, passing range, and football intelligence. His performances at youth level have drawn comparisons to some of the best midfielders in the game, and there is great anticipation about his potential impact on the first team. Patino's development is being closely monitored by the club, and he is expected to be gradually integrated into the senior squad, where he could become a key player in the years to come.

Folarin Balogun

Folarin Balogun is another exciting young talent who has been making waves in Arsenal's youth ranks. A prolific striker with a keen eye for goal, Balogun has shown his ability to find the back of the net at all levels of youth football. His physical presence, speed, and finishing ability have led to comparisons with some of the game's top strikers. Balogun's potential is immense, and as he continues to gain experience, he could become a crucial part of Arsenal's attacking lineup in the future.

These emerging talents, along with others in the academy pipeline, represent the future of Arsenal Football Club. Their development and integration into the first team will be key to Arsenal's long-term success, as the club continues to prioritize youth development and building a team capable of competing at the highest level.

The Vision for Arsenal: Long-Term Strategies and the Club's Vision for the Future

As Arsenal moves forward, the club's long-term vision and strategies are centered around reestablishing itself as one of the leading forces in English and European football. This vision is guided by a commitment to sustainable growth, the development of young talent, and a return to the values and principles that have defined Arsenal's identity for over a century.

Youth Development and Academy Focus

One of the cornerstones of Arsenal's vision for the future is a renewed emphasis on youth development. The club's academy has a storied history of producing world-class talent, and there is a clear strategy in place to continue this tradition. Arsenal aims to identify, nurture, and develop young players who can transition smoothly into the first team and become the backbone of the club's future success. This approach not only ensures a steady pipeline of talent but also aligns with Arsenal's ethos of playing attractive, technically proficient football.

Sustainable Success Through Strategic Recruitment

Arsenal's long-term strategy also includes a focus on strategic recruitment, where the club aims to build a squad capable of competing at the highest levels without relying on excessive spending. This involves identifying players who fit the club's playing philosophy and who have the potential to grow and develop within the team. Arsenal's recruitment policy prioritizes players who can contribute immediately while also having the potential to increase in value over time. The goal is to build a balanced squad that combines experienced professionals with emerging talents, creating a team capable of challenging for domestic and European honors.

Competing for Major Trophies

The ultimate goal for Arsenal is to return to competing regularly for major trophies, including the Premier League and the UEFA Champions League. The club's leadership, under the guidance of Mikel Arteta and technical director Edu, is committed to creating a team that can challenge the best in Europe. This vision involves not only strengthening the squad but also instilling a winning mentality throughout the club. Arsenal's focus on building a cohesive, resilient, and technically gifted team is central to achieving this goal.

Emphasis on Club Values and Culture
Arsenal's vision for the future is deeply rooted in the club's values and culture. The emphasis on playing attractive, attacking football, the commitment to fair play, and the importance of community and social responsibility are all integral to the club's identity. Arsenal aims to be a club that not only wins on the pitch but also makes a positive impact off it. This includes continuing to support community initiatives, promoting diversity and inclusion, and using the club's platform to drive positive change in society.

Infrastructure and Facilities Development
Arsenal is also committed to investing in its infrastructure and facilities to ensure that the club remains at the forefront of modern football. This includes maintaining and enhancing the Emirates Stadium, which remains one of the premier football venues in Europe, as well as investing in state-of-the-art training facilities for both the first team and academy players. These investments are designed to create an environment that fosters excellence and supports the club's long-term ambitions.

Challenges Ahead: Potential Obstacles and Opportunities Facing Arsenal

While Arsenal's vision for the future is ambitious, the club faces several challenges that will need to be addressed to achieve its goals. These challenges, along with potential opportunities, will shape Arsenal's trajectory in the coming years.

Competition in the Premier League and Europe
One of the primary challenges facing Arsenal is the intense competition in both the Premier League and Europe. The financial power of rival clubs, coupled with the increasing quality of teams across the league, means that Arsenal must continuously improve to remain competitive. The challenge is not only to secure a top-four finish and Champions League qualification but also to compete for the Premier League title against well-funded and established rivals like Manchester City, Liverpool, Chelsea, and Manchester United.

Financial Constraints and Sustainability
In the modern football landscape, financial sustainability is crucial. Arsenal must balance the need for investment in the squad with the realities of financial constraints. The club's self-sustaining model, which relies on revenue generated from matchdays, broadcasting, and commercial activities, means that Arsenal must be prudent in its

spending while ensuring that it remains competitive. The challenge is to build a squad capable of winning trophies without compromising the club's financial health.

Retention of Key Players
Retaining key players and fending off interest from other top clubs is another challenge that Arsenal must navigate. As the club develops its young talents and builds a competitive squad, it will be essential to keep hold of its star players. Ensuring that players feel valued and see a clear path to success at Arsenal will be crucial in retaining the core of the team and maintaining stability.

European Competition and the Champions League
Returning to the UEFA Champions League and competing effectively in Europe is a significant challenge and opportunity for Arsenal. The financial and reputational benefits of playing in the Champions League are substantial, and Arsenal's long-term success depends on regular participation in the competition. The challenge lies in securing qualification and then building a team capable of advancing deep into the tournament.

Adapting to Changes in Football
The football landscape is constantly evolving, with changes in technology, fan engagement, and global

markets. Arsenal must be adaptable and innovative to stay ahead of the curve. This includes embracing new technologies, such as data analytics and sports science, to gain a competitive edge, as well as expanding the club's global presence and engaging with fans in new and creative ways.

Opportunities for Growth and Development
Despite the challenges, there are also significant opportunities for Arsenal to grow and develop. The club's global brand, loyal fanbase, and commitment to youth development provide a strong foundation for future success. By continuing to invest in the academy, making smart recruitment decisions, and maintaining a clear vision for the future, Arsenal can capitalize on these opportunities and return to the top of English and European football.

In conclusion, Arsenal's future is filled with both challenges and opportunities. The club's commitment to youth development, sustainable success, and maintaining its core values will be key to navigating the complexities of modern football. With a clear vision and strategic planning, Arsenal can overcome the obstacles ahead and build a team that not only competes for major honors but also upholds the traditions and legacy of one of the most storied clubs in football history.

Appendix A: Complete List of Arsenal Managers

Timeline of Managers

This section provides a chronological list of every manager who has led Arsenal Football Club. For each manager, key details including their tenure, major achievements, and notable contributions to the club are summarized.

1. **Thomas Mitchell (1886-1889)**
   - **Tenure:** 1886-1889
   - **Achievements:** Founding manager during the club's formative years, overseeing the transition from Dial Square to Royal Arsenal.

2. **Henry Norris (1919-1934)**
   - **Tenure:** 1919-1934
   - **Achievements:** Orchestrated Arsenal's promotion to the First Division, oversaw the club's early successes including the first League titles.

3. **Herbert Chapman (1925-1934)**
   - **Tenure:** 1925-1934

- **Achievements:** Introduced the WM formation, led Arsenal to multiple league titles, and revolutionized club tactics and training methods.

4. **George Allison (1934-1947)**

   - **Tenure:** 1934-1947
   - **Achievements:** Continued Chapman's legacy with further league titles, including the 1935 championship and FA Cup victories.

5. **Tom Whittaker (1947-1956)**

   - **Tenure:** 1947-1956
   - **Achievements:** Managed Arsenal to the 1950 FA Cup win and the 1953 league title.

6. **Bertie Mee (1966-1976)**

   - **Tenure:** 1966-1976
   - **Achievements:** Led Arsenal to the 1970-71 Double (FA Cup and League title), and to European success with the Fairs Cup in 1970.

7. **Terry Neill (1976-1983)**
   - **Tenure:** 1976-1983
   - **Achievements:** Guided Arsenal to the 1979 FA Cup victory and consistent cup runs, despite challenges in the league.

8. **Don Howe (1983-1986)**
   - **Tenure:** 1983-1986
   - **Achievements:** Served as caretaker manager and then as head coach, contributing to the club's tactical approaches.

9. **George Graham (1986-1995)**
   - **Tenure:** 1986-1995
   - **Achievements:** Oversaw Arsenal's first league title in 18 years in 1989, and a second in 1991, as well as winning the FA Cup and the League Cup.

10. **Bruce Rioch (1995-1996)**
    - **Tenure:** 1995-1996
    - **Achievements:** Managed Arsenal to a 5th place finish in the Premier League

and reached the semi-finals of the UEFA Cup.

11. **Arsène Wenger (1996-2018)**

    - **Tenure:** 1996-2018
    - **Achievements:** Transformed Arsenal with innovative tactics, led the team to an unbeaten league season in 2003-2004, and won multiple FA Cups.

12. **Unai Emery (2018-2019)**

    - **Tenure:** 2018-2019
    - **Achievements:** Reached the Europa League final, though struggled with league performance.

13. **Mikel Arteta (2019-Present)**

    - **Tenure:** 2019-Present
    - **Achievements:** Secured the FA Cup in his first season and is building a team with a focus on youth and attacking style.

Impact Analysis

This section explores the influence of each manager on Arsenal FC, detailing how their strategies, philosophies, and leadership styles have shaped the club's history and direction.

1. **Thomas Mitchell**
   - **Impact:** As the founding manager, Mitchell set the foundation for Arsenal's early development, guiding the transition from Dial Square to Royal Arsenal and establishing the club's early identity.

2. **Henry Norris**
   - **Impact:** Norris played a crucial role in Arsenal's entry into the Football League's First Division and set the stage for future successes through strategic investments and infrastructure improvements.

3. **Herbert Chapman**
   - **Impact:** Chapman's innovative tactics, including the WM formation, and focus on professionalism revolutionized English football. His influence led to significant domestic success and laid the groundwork for Arsenal's modern era.

4. **George Allison**

    o **Impact:** Allison built on Chapman's legacy, maintaining Arsenal's dominance in English football with additional league titles and a successful FA Cup campaign, cementing the club's status as a top competitor.

5. **Tom Whittaker**

    o **Impact:** Whittaker's tenure was marked by stability and success, with notable victories that preserved Arsenal's position as a leading club and set up the team for future triumphs.

6. **Bertie Mee**

    o **Impact:** Mee's era is remembered for the successful Double in 1971 and the Fairs Cup win, revitalizing Arsenal and establishing a new era of competitiveness and success in both domestic and European football.

7. **Terry Neill**

    o **Impact:** Neill managed to secure the 1979 FA Cup and maintained Arsenal's prominence, though his tenure faced challenges. His leadership was crucial during a transitional period for the club.

8. **Don Howe**
    - **Impact:** Howe's contributions to Arsenal were marked by tactical advancements and coaching expertise. His influence was integral in preparing the club for the future leadership of George Graham.

9. **George Graham**
    - **Impact:** Graham's emphasis on defensive solidity and tactical discipline brought Arsenal significant success, including memorable league titles and domestic cups. His legacy includes the establishment of a formidable defensive unit.

10. **Bruce Rioch**
    - **Impact:** Rioch's brief tenure was characterized by efforts to build a competitive squad, though his time was marred by inconsistent results and his inability to secure long-term success.

11. **Arsène Wenger**
    - **Impact:** Wenger's revolutionary approach to football, focusing on attacking play and youth development, reshaped Arsenal and English football. His tenure brought an unbeaten league season and multiple FA Cups, leaving a lasting legacy on the club's philosophy and style.

12. **Unai Emery**
    - **Impact:** Emery's focus on European competitions saw Arsenal reach the Europa League final. His tenure was a period of transition, facing challenges in integrating his strategies within the Premier League.

13. **Mikel Arteta**
    - **Impact:** Arteta's appointment has marked a period of rebuilding and rejuvenation. His focus on youth and tactical flexibility has already brought silverware and promises to reshape Arsenal's future direction.

Appendix B: Complete List of Arsenal Managers

Timeline of Managers: A List of Every Arsenal Manager and Their Records

Arsenal Football Club has been guided by a diverse range of managers throughout its storied history. Each manager brought their own philosophy and approach, contributing to the club's evolution. Below is a chronological list of every Arsenal manager, detailing their tenure, records, and significant achievements.

1. **Thomas Mitchell (1897-1898)**
   - **Tenure:** 1897-1898
   - **Record:** N/A
   - **Achievements:** First manager of Arsenal (then Woolwich Arsenal), laying the groundwork for professional management.

2. **Sam Hollis (1898-1899)**
   - **Tenure:** 1898-1899
   - **Record:** N/A
   - **Achievements:** Managed during the early Football League years, continuing the club's professional development.

3. **George Elcoat (1899-1900)**

    o **Tenure:** 1899-1900

    o **Record:** N/A

    o **Achievements:** Oversaw a period of stabilization as the club solidified its status in professional football.

4. **Harry Bradshaw (1901-1904)**

    o **Tenure:** 1901-1904

    o **Record:** N/A

    o **Achievements:** Led Arsenal to significant progress, setting the stage for future success.

5. **Phil Kelso (1904-1908)**

    o **Tenure:** 1904-1908

    o **Record:** N/A

    o **Achievements:** Managed Arsenal during its early First Division years, helping the club establish itself in the top tier.

6. **George Morrell (1908-1915)**
    - **Tenure:** 1908-1915
    - **Record:** N/A
    - **Achievements:** Guided the club through financial difficulties and World War I, maintaining its league status.

7. **Leslie Knighton (1919-1925)**
    - **Tenure:** 1919-1925
    - **Record:** N/A
    - **Achievements:** Rebuilt the team post-World War I, keeping Arsenal competitive in the league.

8. **Herbert Chapman (1925-1934)**
    - **Tenure:** 1925-1934
    - **Record:** 403 matches, 201 wins, 106 draws, 96 losses
    - **Achievements:** 2 League Titles (1930-31, 1932-33), 1 FA Cup (1930); revolutionized football tactics and management, establishing Arsenal as a powerhouse.

9. **Joe Shaw (1934, caretaker)**

    o **Tenure:** 1934 (caretaker)

    o **Record:** 23 matches, 15 wins, 4 draws, 4 losses

    o **Achievements:** Guided Arsenal to the 1933-34 league title after Chapman's sudden death.

10. **George Allison (1934-1947)**

    o **Tenure:** 1934-1947

    o **Record:** 429 matches, 202 wins, 116 draws, 111 losses

    o **Achievements:** 2 League Titles (1934-35, 1937-38), 1 FA Cup (1936); managed the club through World War II, maintaining competitive success.

11. **Tom Whittaker (1947-1956)**

    o **Tenure:** 1947-1956

    o **Record:** 430 matches, 196 wins, 107 draws, 127 losses

    o **Achievements:** 2 League Titles (1947-48, 1952-53), 1 FA Cup (1950);

successfully continued Arsenal's dominance in the post-war era.

12. **Jack Crayston (1956-1958)**
    - **Tenure:** 1956-1958
    - **Record:** 77 matches, 37 wins, 18 draws, 22 losses
    - **Achievements:** Stabilized the club during a transitional period.

13. **George Swindin (1958-1962)**
    - **Tenure:** 1958-1962
    - **Record:** 179 matches, 75 wins, 39 draws, 65 losses
    - **Achievements:** Built a competitive squad, though without securing major silverware.

14. **Billy Wright (1962-1966)**
    - **Tenure:** 1962-1966
    - **Record:** 182 matches, 73 wins, 39 draws, 70 losses
    - **Achievements:** Focused on youth development, setting the stage for future talents despite a lack of trophies.

15. **Bertie Mee (1966-1976)**

    - **Tenure:** 1966-1976
    - **Record:** 539 matches, 241 wins, 142 draws, 156 losses
    - **Achievements:** 1 League Title (1970-71), 1 FA Cup (1971), 1 Inter-Cities Fairs Cup (1970); oversaw Arsenal's first Double.

16. **Terry Neill (1976-1983)**

    - **Tenure:** 1976-1983
    - **Record:** 416 matches, 187 wins, 119 draws, 110 losses
    - **Achievements:** Led Arsenal to 3 FA Cup finals, winning in 1979; guided the club through a competitive era.

17. **Don Howe (1983-1986)**

    - **Tenure:** 1983-1986
    - **Record:** 117 matches, 46 wins, 34 draws, 37 losses
    - **Achievements:** Rebuilt the squad and laid the groundwork for future success.

18. **Steve Burtenshaw (1986, caretaker)**
    - **Tenure:** 1986 (caretaker)
    - **Record:** 11 matches, 3 wins, 4 draws, 4 losses
    - **Achievements:** Provided interim leadership before the appointment of George Graham.

19. **George Graham (1986-1995)**
    - **Tenure:** 1986-1995
    - **Record:** 460 matches, 225 wins, 127 draws, 108 losses
    - **Achievements:** 2 League Titles (1988-89, 1990-91), 2 FA Cups (1993), 1 League Cup (1987), 1 European Cup Winners' Cup (1994); known for defensive solidity and tactical discipline.

20. **Stewart Houston (1995, caretaker)**
    - **Tenure:** 1995 (caretaker)
    - **Record:** 17 matches, 7 wins, 3 draws, 7 losses
    - **Achievements:** Led Arsenal to the Cup Winners' Cup final as interim manager.

21. **Bruce Rioch (1995-1996)**

    o **Tenure:** 1995-1996

    o **Record:** 47 matches, 22 wins, 15 draws, 10 losses

    o **Achievements:** Secured UEFA Cup qualification and signed Dennis Bergkamp, laying the groundwork for future success.

22. **Stewart Houston (1996, caretaker)**

    o **Tenure:** 1996 (caretaker)

    o **Record:** 12 matches, 6 wins, 4 draws, 2 losses

    o **Achievements:** Managed the club during a transitional phase before Wenger's appointment.

23. **Pat Rice (1996, caretaker)**

    o **Tenure:** 1996 (caretaker)

    o **Record:** 4 matches, 3 wins, 0 draws, 1 loss

    o **Achievements:** Brief caretaker role before Wenger's era began.

24. **Arsène Wenger (1996-2018)**
    - **Tenure:** 1996-2018
    - **Record:** 1,235 matches, 707 wins, 280 draws, 248 losses
    - **Achievements:** 3 Premier League Titles (1997-98, 2001-02, 2003-04), 7 FA Cups, Invincibles season (2003-04); transformed Arsenal into a modern football powerhouse and led the move to Emirates Stadium.

25. **Unai Emery (2018-2019)**
    - **Tenure:** 2018-2019
    - **Record:** 78 matches, 43 wins, 15 draws, 20 losses
    - **Achievements:** Reached the UEFA Europa League final (2019); began the process of transitioning from Wenger's long tenure.

26. **Freddie Ljungberg (2019, caretaker)**
    - **Tenure:** 2019 (caretaker)
    - **Record:** 6 matches, 1 win, 3 draws, 2 losses

- **Achievements:** Provided stability during a difficult period before Arteta's arrival.

27. **Mikel Arteta (2019-present)**

    - **Tenure:** 2019-present
    - **Record:** Ongoing
    - **Achievements:** 1 FA Cup (2020), 1 Community Shield (2020); working on rebuilding the squad and returning Arsenal to the top of English and European football.

Impact Analysis: The Influence of Each Manager on the Club's Direction

Herbert Chapman (1925-1934):

Chapman is widely recognized as a transformative figure in Arsenal's history. His innovations in tactics, training, and management revolutionized the club and English football as a whole. Chapman's vision laid the foundation for Arsenal's dominance in the 1930s and established a legacy of excellence that would influence future generations.

George Allison (1934-1947):

Allison successfully continued Chapman's work, guiding Arsenal through challenging times, including World War II. His ability to maintain the club's competitive edge during these years ensured that Arsenal remained a major force in English football.

Tom Whittaker (1947-1956):

Whittaker carried forward the success of the Chapman-Allison era, securing league titles and maintaining Arsenal's status as one of England's top clubs. His tenure is remembered for the continuation of Arsenal's winning tradition in the post-war period.

George Graham (1986-1995):

Graham restored Arsenal's competitiveness in the late 1980s and early 1990s, with a focus on defensive solidity and discipline. His teams were known for their organization and resilience, and Graham's success in both domestic and European competitions reinforced Arsenal's reputation as a top club.

Arsène Wenger (1996-2018):

Wenger's influence on Arsenal is unparalleled. His arrival marked a new era of attacking football, youth development, and internationalization. Wenger's emphasis on technical skill and innovation transformed Arsenal into a global brand and led to some of the most successful periods in the club's history. His legacy is not only in the trophies won but in the cultural shift he brought to the club and English football.

Mikel Arteta (2019-present):

Arteta's tenure represents a new chapter in Arsenal's history, focused on rebuilding and returning to the club's core values. His early success in winning the FA Cup and Community Shield has been followed by a long-term project aimed at restoring Arsenal's competitiveness in the Premier League and Europe. Arteta's leadership and vision are crucial to shaping the future direction of the club.

Appendix C: Arsenal in European Competitions

European Campaigns: A Summary of Arsenal's Performance in European Tournaments

Arsenal Football Club has a rich history of competing in European tournaments, where the team has experienced both triumphs and heartbreaks. This section provides a summary of Arsenal's performance across the major European competitions, including the UEFA Champions League, UEFA Europa League, and the now-defunct UEFA Cup Winners' Cup.

UEFA Champions League (1998-Present) Arsenal first qualified for the UEFA Champions League under Arsène Wenger in the 1998-99 season, marking the beginning of a long and consistent presence in Europe's premier club competition. Arsenal enjoyed numerous successful campaigns, consistently reaching the knockout stages, with their peak coming in the 2005-06 season when they reached the final. Despite leading for much of the match, Arsenal lost 2-1 to Barcelona after a late comeback by the Catalan side. This remains the closest Arsenal has come to lifting the Champions League trophy.

UEFA Europa League (2000-Present) The UEFA Europa League, formerly known as the

UEFA Cup, has seen Arsenal compete with varying degrees of success. Arsenal reached the final of the Europa League in the 2018-19 season under Unai Emery, a competition specialist. However, they were defeated 4-1 by Chelsea in an all-English final. Arsenal has also made deep runs in the competition under Mikel Arteta, aiming to use the Europa League as a pathway back to the Champions League.

UEFA Cup Winners' Cup (1963-1999)
The UEFA Cup Winners' Cup was a competition for domestic cup winners across Europe, and Arsenal's most significant triumph in this tournament came in 1994. Under George Graham, Arsenal defeated Parma 1-0 in the final, with Alan Smith scoring the decisive goal. This victory marked Arsenal's second European trophy, following their Fairs Cup win in 1970. The competition was abolished in 1999, with many of the teams merging into the UEFA Cup, later rebranded as the Europa League.

Inter-Cities Fairs Cup (1955-1971)
Before the establishment of the UEFA Cup, Arsenal won their first major European honor in the form of the Inter-Cities Fairs Cup in 1970. Arsenal defeated Anderlecht 4-3 on aggregate in the final, marking a significant achievement in the club's history. This

victory was a springboard for further domestic success in the early 1970s.

Significant Matches: Key Games That Defined Arsenal's European History

Throughout Arsenal's history in European competitions, several matches have stood out as defining moments. These games not only highlighted Arsenal's quality but also left a lasting impact on the club's European legacy.

Arsenal 3-0 Anderlecht (1970 Inter-Cities Fairs Cup Final, Second Leg)

This match is one of the most significant in Arsenal's European history. Trailing 3-1 from the first leg in Belgium, Arsenal needed a strong performance at Highbury to overturn the deficit. The Gunners responded with a resounding 3-0 victory, securing a 4-3 aggregate win to claim their first European trophy. Goals from John Radford, Eddie Kelly, and Jon Sammels completed the comeback, and the match is remembered as a turning point in Arsenal's history, ending a 17-year wait for silverware.

Arsenal 1-0 Parma (1994 UEFA Cup Winners' Cup Final)

Arsenal's victory in the 1994 UEFA Cup Winners' Cup final is one of the club's greatest European achievements. Facing a strong Parma side featuring the likes of Gianfranco Zola and Faustino Asprilla, Arsenal were the underdogs. However, a first-half strike from Alan Smith secured a famous 1-0 win. The match was notable for Arsenal's resolute defensive display, with the backline, led by Tony Adams, and goalkeeper David Seaman, playing crucial roles in securing the trophy.

Arsenal 2-1 Real Madrid (2006 UEFA Champions League Round of 16, Second Leg)

In the 2005-06 UEFA Champions League campaign, Arsenal faced Real Madrid in the Round of 16. After a memorable 1-0 victory at the Santiago Bernabéu in the first leg, thanks to a Thierry Henry goal, Arsenal returned to Highbury to complete the job. A tense 0-0 draw in the second leg saw Arsenal progress to the quarter-finals, marking the first time an English club had eliminated Real Madrid from the Champions League. This victory was a significant milestone in Arsenal's run to the final that year.

Arsenal 1-2 Barcelona (2006 UEFA Champions League Final)

The 2006 Champions League final remains one of the most heartbreaking moments in Arsenal's European history. Arsenal took the lead through Sol Campbell, despite being reduced to 10 men after Jens Lehmann's early red card. However, Barcelona scored twice in the final 15 minutes, denying

Arsenal their first Champions League title. The match is remembered for Arsenal's valiant effort and remains a poignant moment in the club's European journey.

Arsenal 7-0 Slavia Prague (2007 UEFA Champions League Group Stage)
One of Arsenal's most dominant performances in European competition came in the 2007-08 Champions League group stage. Arsenal dismantled Slavia Prague 7-0 at the Emirates Stadium, showcasing the attacking prowess of a team that included Cesc Fàbregas, Theo Walcott, and Emmanuel Adebayor. The victory remains Arsenal's largest win in European competition and a highlight of their time in the Champions League.

Arsenal 3-1 Valencia (2019 UEFA Europa League Semi-Final, First Leg)
In the 2018-19 Europa League semi-final, Arsenal faced Valencia in a crucial tie. The first leg at the Emirates Stadium saw Arsenal come from behind to win 3-1, with Alexandre Lacazette scoring twice and Pierre-Emerick Aubameyang adding a third. This result set the stage for a 4-2 win in the second leg, securing Arsenal's place in the final. Although Arsenal would ultimately lose the final to Chelsea, this semi-final performance was a testament to the

team's resilience and attacking quality under Unai Emery.

These significant matches reflect the highs and lows of Arsenal's European campaigns, capturing moments of triumph, heartbreak, and brilliance that have defined the club's journey on the continental stage. Arsenal's history in Europe is a testament to the club's ambition and enduring quest for glory, as they continue to strive for success in the most prestigious tournaments in football.

Bibliography and References

Books

1. **Hornby, Nick. *Fever Pitch*. London: Victor Gollancz, 1992.**
   - A seminal work on football fandom that includes deep reflections on supporting Arsenal and the culture surrounding the club.

2. **Soar, Phil, and Tyler, Martin. *The Official Illustrated History of Arsenal 1886-2014*. London: Hamlyn, 2014.**
   - A comprehensive official history of Arsenal, detailing the club's journey from its foundation to the modern era.

3. **Collins, Tony, and Phelps, Matthew. *Arsenal: The Complete Record*. Derby: Breedon Books, 2007.**
   - An exhaustive compilation of Arsenal's match records, player statistics, and historical milestones.

4. **Graham, George. *The Glory & The Grief: The Inside Story of Arsenal Under George Graham*. London: Mainstream Publishing, 1997.**

- An insider account of Arsenal's successes and challenges during George Graham's tenure as manager.

5. **Chapman, Herbert.** *Herbert Chapman on Football.* **London: Faber & Faber, 1934.**

    - Insights from one of football's most influential managers, offering a glimpse into the philosophy that shaped modern Arsenal.

6. **Wenger, Arsène.** *My Life in Red and White: My Autobiography.* **London: W&N, 2020.**

    - Arsène Wenger's autobiography, providing a personal account of his time at Arsenal and his vision for the club.

7. **Spurling, Jon.** *Rebels for the Cause: The Alternative History of Arsenal Football Club.* **Edinburgh: Mainstream Publishing, 2004.**

    - An alternative history of Arsenal, exploring the club's culture, fans, and the controversies that have shaped its identity.

8. **Harris, Jeff, and Hogg, Tony.** *Arsenal Who's Who.* **Edinburgh: Mainstream Publishing, 1995.**

- A comprehensive guide to the players, managers, and key figures in Arsenal's history.

9. **Joyce, Michael.** *Football League Players' Records 1888 to 1939.* **Nottingham: Tony Brown, 2004.**

    - An authoritative source on early football players, including those who contributed to Arsenal's rise in the early 20th century.

Articles and Journals

1. **Taylor, Matthew. "The Global Diffusion of Sports: The Case of English Football in Europe, 1870-1939."** *Journal of Historical Sociology* **19, no. 4 (2006): 442-463.**

    - A scholarly article exploring the early spread of football across Europe, including Arsenal's role in this process.

2. **Barker, Philip. "Arsenal and the Birth of Modern Football."** *Soccer & Society* **12, no. 3 (2011): 303-320.**

    - An analysis of Arsenal's contribution to the development of modern football tactics and management.

3. **Conn, David. "Arsenal's Move to the Emirates: Financial Insights and Future Prospects."** *The Guardian,* **March 9, 2006.**

    - A journalistic investigation into the financial and strategic implications of Arsenal's move to the Emirates Stadium.

4. **Glendenning, Barry. "The Invincibles: A Season in Review."** *The Guardian,* **May 18, 2004.**

    - A detailed review of Arsenal's unbeaten 2003-2004 Premier League season, offering insights into the team's performance and legacy.

Official Documents and Reports

1. **Arsenal Football Club.** *Annual Reports and Financial Statements.* **London: Arsenal Holdings plc, Various Years.**

    - Official financial statements and reports that provide insights into the club's economic health and strategic decisions over the years.

2. **UEFA.** *UEFA Competitions Historical Archive.* **Nyon: Union of European Football Associations, 2023.**

- A comprehensive archive of UEFA competitions, including Arsenal's participation and performances in European tournaments.

3. **Premier League.** *Premier League Handbook.* **London: Premier League, Various Years.**

    - The official handbook of the Premier League, detailing rules, regulations, and historical records relevant to Arsenal's participation.

Interviews and Oral Histories

1. **Wenger, Arsène. "In Conversation: Arsène Wenger." Interview by Gary Lineker.** *BBC Sport,* **November 2020.**

    - An interview offering insights into Wenger's philosophy and reflections on his time at Arsenal.

2. **Adams, Tony. "Tony Adams on Leadership and Arsenal's Glory Years." Interview by John Cross.** *Daily Mirror,* **August 2017.**

    - A reflective interview with Tony Adams discussing his role in Arsenal's successes and the challenges he faced.

3. **Henry, Thierry. "The Making of a Legend: Thierry Henry Reflects on His Arsenal Career." Interview by Amy Lawrence.** *The Athletic,* **February 2021.**

    o Thierry Henry shares his experiences at Arsenal, offering a personal perspective on his achievements and the club's evolution.

Websites and Online Resources

1. **Arsenal.com.** *The Official Arsenal Website.*

    o The official website of Arsenal Football Club, offering news, historical archives, and information on current and past teams.

2. **Transfermarkt. "Arsenal FC Historical Transfers." Transfermarkt GmbH & Co. KG, 2023.**

    o A database providing detailed records of Arsenal's player transfers, statistics, and career summaries.

3. **Soccerbase. "Arsenal Results Archive." Centurycomm Limited, 2023.**

- An online archive of Arsenal's match results, player statistics, and historical data.

4. **BBC Sport. "Arsenal: Club History and Records." BBC, 2023.**

    - A dedicated section on Arsenal's history, featuring articles, statistics, and key moments in the club's history.

Archival Material

1. **British Library Newspaper Archive.** *Arsenal Football Club Reports (1886-2023).* **London: British Library.**

    - A collection of historical newspaper reports and articles detailing Arsenal's matches, management decisions, and cultural impact.

2. **London Metropolitan Archives.** *Arsenal Football Club Records.* **London: City of London Corporation.**

    - A repository of historical documents, minutes, and official records related to the governance and operation of Arsenal Football Club.

3. **National Football Museum.** *Herbert Chapman Papers.* **Manchester: National Football Museum.**

    ○ Archival material related to Herbert Chapman, including personal correspondence, tactical notes, and management strategies.

www.ingramcontent.com/pod-product-compliance
Ingram Content Group UK Ltd.
Pitfield, Milton Keynes, MK11 3LW, UK
UKHW020710220925
8009UKWH00042B/616